SHARING CHRIST

Giving the Eternal Gift

Sharing Christ: Giving the Eternal Gift

Published by
New*Life* Publications
A ministry of Campus Crusade for Christ
375 Highway 74 South, Suite A
Peachtree City, GA 30269

© 2004, New*Life* Publications. All rights reserved. No part of this book may be reproduced, stored in a retrieval system, or transmitted in any form or by any means, except in the case of brief quotations printed in articles or reviews, without prior permission in writing from the publisher.

Design and production by Genesis Group

Cover by Koechel Peterson & Assoc., Minneapolis, MN

Printed in the United States of America

ISBN 1-56399-209-4

Unless otherwise indicated, all Scripture quotations are from *The Living Bible*, © 1971 by Tyndale House Publishers, Wheaton, IL 60187. All rights reserved.

Scripture quotations designated NKJ are from the *New King James* version, © 1979, 1980, 1982 by Thomas Nelson Inc., Publishers, Nashville, Tennessee.

Scripture quotations designated NIV are from the *New International Version*, © 1973, 1978, 1984 by the International Bible Society. Published by Zondervan Bible Publishers, Grand Rapids, Michigan.

CONTENTS

Foreword *by Josh McDowell* 5
Introduction 7
1 You Can Do It! 9
2 Success in Witnessing 21
3 The Love of Christ Compels Us 33
4 Barriers to Witnessing 47
5 Preparation for Witnessing 59
6 Sharing the Good News 77
7 Helping Others Grow in Their Faith 97

Would You Like to Know God Personally? . . .*115*
Resources *125*

This book, part of the Bill Bright *Signature Series*, is a condensation of *Witnessing Without Fear*, which was published in 1993 and re-issued in 2003.

As Members of
Global Founding Partners

the following families are helping to fulfill the Great Commission through helping to train Millions of Pastors around the world.

Bill and Christie Heavener and Family
Ed and Edye Haddock and Family
Stuart and Debbie Sue Irby and Family

FOREWORD

PARTICIPATING WITH God in introducing others to Christ is our greatest commission and our greatest privilege. Unfortunately, it is also often our greatest fear. Even long-time Christians struggle with fears in sharing their faith. We fear that we are inadequate to participate in this awesome task. We fear that we will make a mistake, say the wrong words, and turn someone off. We fear that we will offend people or lose friends who aren't open to hearing what we have to say.

Still, the Scriptures instruct us to be prepared, "always being ready to make a defense to everyone who asks you to give an account for the hope that is in you" (1 Peter 3:15, NASB). One of the greatest examples I have known of a man who is always prepared to share his faith is my friend and mentor, Bill Bright. Evangelism is such a way of life with him, and whenever people are around him, they walk away with a greater desire to talk to people about the Lord.

SHARING CHRIST

It has been a burning desire of mine that every believer could spend time one on one with a man like Bill Bright. *Witnessing Without Fear* is the next best thing. In this book, Bill Bright has recorded his insight into our holy task of sharing the faith. In his own unique style, he presents our calling to join God in making disciples. He gives practical instruction on praying for nonbelievers and talking to them about the Lord in simple, compelling terms. He even takes us into the next step of discipling those who have trusted Christ.

Years ago, I read this book for the first time. Bill's insights into evangelism have given me more courage and know-how to share my faith than anything I have ever read apart from the Scriptures. Witnessing without fear is truly a reality in my life, and I'm grateful to Bill for writing this book to share his passion for evangelism.

The book you are holding in your hands is a powerful tool that will help better prepare you for the Lord's work. Be ready to see exciting changes in your own life and in the lives of those around you as you share your faith with confidence!

Until the whole world hears,

JOSH D. MCDOWELL

INTRODUCTION

HAVE YOU TALKED with anyone about Jesus Christ during the past week? During the past month? In the past year? Since you became a Christian?

Since 1945 I have been involved in helping to train Christians across the country and around the world to share their faith in Christ more effectively. While I am encouraged that numerous Christians are beginning to witness with confidence, studies still show that the vast majority of believers—perhaps up to 98 percent—are neither confident nor effective in their witness for our Savior.

There are several reasons why Christians don't witness, which we will address in this book. But the tragedy is that in failing to share one's faith, a Christian misses out on one of the greatest blessings our Lord offers: the profound joy of helping a fellow human being find new, abundant life, as well as eternal life, in Jesus Christ.

Most Christians, we've found, really *do* want to know how to give a clear, effective presentation

SHARING CHRIST

of the gospel, but lack the practical know-how. If you are among them, I've prepared this book especially for you, to help you learn to share your faith with confidence.

The principles you are about to study have been learned in the crucible of front-line experience. In training conferences around the world, this information has changed multitudes of silent, guilt-ridden Christians into radiant witnesses for our Lord. Every story in this book is true, although in most cases I have changed or withheld the names of people involved out of respect for their privacy.

If you apply the proven concepts presented in the following pages, you, too, will become more effective in sharing Christ with your family, friends, neighbors, coworkers, and casual acquaintances.

I am praying for you—that as a result of your study of these concepts, you will receive new confidence and joy in telling others of our wonderful Lord and Savior, Jesus Christ...and that God will enable you to introduce many men and women to Him.

YOU CAN DO IT!

IF I COULD SHOW you how you can share your faith successfully, and with confidence--without alienating others or becoming someone you really don't want to be—would you be interested?

Witnessing for our Lord is something we all know we should do. From the pulpit on Sunday mornings we hear that we should "spread the Word in the marketplace." In our Christian magazines and books we read that our neighbors are hungry for the gospel—in fact, they are dying without Christ. In God's Word we read the command of Jesus Himself to "go into all the world and preach the gospel to every creature."

Yet, witnessing is an activity from which most Christians frequently shrink. To intrude in someone else's life seems not only threatening but blatantly presumptuous. We fear offending the other person, fear being rejected, fear doing an inadequate job of representing our Lord, and even being branded a "fanatic."

SHARING CHRIST

So we remain silent, and pray that God will use someone else to get His message to those around us who do not know Him.

If you, too, have struggled with these fears, I have good news for you!

Christians just like you, from all walks of life, are learning how to share their faith in Christ effectively. Let me tell you about just a few of them.

"It Almost Seemed Too Simple"

Steve and Jackie became Christians after they were married. As they grew in their faith, they saw positive changes in several key areas of their lives, but one area that frustrated them was their inability to talk with people about their relationship with Jesus Christ.

"Then a friend suggested we attend a Lay Institute for Evangelism, designed for Christians who want to be more effective in sharing their faith," Steve relates. "Jackie and I thought, *What have we got to lose?*"

At the conference, Steve and Jackie learned how to be filled with the Holy Spirit and how to witness for Christ using a very simple presentation of the gospel. "It almost seemed too simple," Steve says, "but since this method had proven effective for others, we decided to give it a try."

Soon, Jackie had led one of her neighbors to Christ, and was meeting regularly with her for follow-up Bible study and fellowship. A short while later, Steve had the privilege of leading his mother and Jackie's father to the Lord. Now they feel confident in witnessing to friends, business acquaintances, and even people they've just met. They have introduced many others to Christ since they received those few hours of training in basic evangelism.

From Shy Introvert to Bold Witness

Al, a school custodian in Florida, says he has been an introvert most of his life. But "the Lord did a miracle" in his life a few years ago to give him the confidence he needed to tell others about Jesus.

"I would sit back and let somebody else do the work of reaching people for Christ," Al says. "But in 1980 my church sponsored a course in evangelism, which I attended. One of the men there, who had seen my faithfulness in helping with the church visitation program, asked me to come with him to a prison outreach.

"I went, and at the prison I engaged a guy in conversation. I asked him if he'd like to receive

SHARING CHRIST

Jesus as his Savior—and he said yes! It floored me! I explained the gospel to him, and he became the first person who actually received Christ with me."

Now, Al shares his faith readily, as a natural part of his life. And people are responding. "One weekend the school where I work held a bazaar, and they had arranged for chicken dinners. At 8 A.M. on Friday a truck pulled up with six cases of chicken, and as I took the delivery guy to the refrigerator, I sensed the Lord telling me to ask him, 'Have you experienced the joy of knowing God personally?'

Now, Al shares his faith readily, as a natural part of his life. And people are responding.

"He said no. I explained the gospel to him, and fifteen minutes later, as we were standing together in the parking lot, he invited Christ into his life. The Lord had prepared him—it was just a matter of my bringing up the subject."

With just a small amount of training in how to witness, Al had changed from a shy introvert to a bold witness for the Lord Jesus. And his sharing of his faith has been effective—hundreds of people in Jacksonville have been transformed as a result of Al's confident witness.

You Can Do It!

Sharing "The Most Important Thing in My Life"

Jill, a Minneapolis homemaker, wanted to somehow affect her neighborhood with God's love, but she became fearful every time she contemplated how to go about it. Then a friend, Joyce, a Campus Crusade staff member with experience in personal evangelism, offered to give an evangelistic Christmas coffee in Jill's home.

Jill agreed, but was so apprehensive that she made Joyce promise not to make her do anything but serve the food. "I don't know how my neighbors will take this," Jill explained nervously.

When the coffee was over and the guests were preparing to leave, Jill spoke up. "May I just say something?" she asked, as tears of love came to her eyes. "I have lived in this neighborhood for five years, and I've dreamed of having you all in my home. I've also dreamed of sharing the most important thing in my life with you, and that's my relationship with Jesus Christ. Apart from this opportunity, I wouldn't have done it."

As tears streamed down Jill's face, the fifteen neighborhood women were crying, too. A real, ongoing ministry in the lives of those women began on that day as the Lord changed Jill from an

SHARING CHRIST

uneasy observer to a bold communicator of God's love.

Trusting God with the Results

Burt, a surgeon in Wisconsin, taught an adult Sunday school class, counseled drug addicts, and had led several people to the Lord. He attended one of our Christian seminars for executives feeling "rather self-complacent, fully expecting to counsel others rather than to be helped myself."

Part of the seminar dealt with how to reach others for Christ through a simple, straightforward presentation of the gospel. Burt determined that he would begin sharing Christ with each of his patients, "even if I just handed them a booklet explaining the gospel with the remark that it had been meaningful in my life. As I did so, I received some terrific responses."

Encouraged at his newfound effectiveness in witnessing, Burt decided to use these same methods in another arena. "I also work at the Addiction Center in my city, counseling heroin addicts. Before the seminar I saw only haphazard results when I presented Christ as the only means of healing. I was trying hard in my own efforts and failing miserably.

You Can Do It!

"After the seminar I decided to present a simple gospel message and trust God with the results. When I asked a young man if he had ever investigated Christ's claims, he said he had been to church and rejected the whole thing. But when I asked him if he had actually done any investigating, he had to say no. I shared the gospel with him, and he prayed with me, receiving Christ into his life.

"At my suggestion he got a modern translation of the Bible. This aroused his mother's curiosity, and she came in to see me. When I told her that her son had become a Christian, tears came to her eyes, and she said that this was the answer to years of prayer."

"I am seeing consistent results as others respond to God's love through my witness."

Burt reports that, since the seminar, "I am seeing consistent results as others respond to God's love through my witness."

Led Her Neighbor to Christ

Kathy, a young commercial artist from Denver, was having a friendly visit with her next-door neighbor, Sue, when the subject of personal value systems came up. Kathy explained how, as a Christian, her value system was centered around Jesus Christ and the Bible.

"I've wondered about those things," Sue replied. "But they've never seemed very real to me. My only view of Christianity has been of 'religious fanatics,' but you don't seem to fit that mold."

Because Kathy had received our basic training in evangelism, she was able to give her neighbor a simple, non-threatening presentation of what Christianity was all about. Right there, in Kathy's back yard, Sue received Christ into her life. She and her husband now attend a thriving church in the area and are active in a couples' Bible study.

Not a "Born Natural" at Witnessing

Like many of these people, I have never found witnessing to come naturally and easily. Some of you may find this difficult to believe, but by nature I'm a shy, reserved person; initiating conversations with strangers is sometimes difficult for me. Even sharing the greatest news ever announced —that "God so loved the world that He gave His only begotten Son, that whoever believes in Him should not perish but have everlasting life"—is not always as easy for me as you might imagine.

So it might seem incongruous that God called

a shy young man in 1951 to launch an evangelistic ministry on the campus of UCLA, a ministry which would become Campus Crusade for Christ International. Witnessing, and training laypeople to witness, is our primary calling. I don't even know if evangelism is my spiritual gift.

What I do know is that God has made it crystal clear in His Word that every Christian is to "go and make disciples in all the nations,...and then teach these new disciples to obey all the commands I have given you" (Matthew 28:19,20). I've tried to be obedient to this command, and God has honored my obedience. Like the people whose true stories I've shared in these pages, God has transformed my personal witness from one of shy hesitancy to one of confident initiative.

If He can do it for me, and for Steve and Jackie, Al, Jill, Burt, Kathy, and millions of others who have learned the important principles in this book, He can do it for you, too.

Never again will you need to be afraid that you'll be embarrassed in a witnessing situation.

Never again will you lack the essential Scriptures and key thoughts to share with an interested listener.

You'll find it more and more natural to begin

SHARING CHRIST

a conversation about Jesus.

You'll know how to handle questions, distractions, even objections.

You'll learn how to guide a person to a definite commitment to our Lord Jesus Christ.

And how to help the new believer begin to grow in his new walk with God.

If you're thinking at this point that "it may work for someone else, but not for me," you're not alone. We have seen thousands of Christians enter into this training totally convinced that it was not for them: it was too simple, they were too shy, or we "didn't know their situation." But they emerged from the training with their spirits rejoicing that God had transformed *their* witness, too, from shyness or complacency to confident initiative.

God will do the same for you.

Study the principles of this book with an open, eager mind.

As you read, continually pray that God will show you how to apply these principles in your own situation.

Practice the concepts you learn with a Christian friend. (Or, if God so leads, with a nonbeliever. We have heard many testimonies of how Christians have practiced these ideas with non-Christian friends, and the nonbelievers received Christ as their Savior and Lord on the spot.)

Begin to apply what you learn on a daily basis, just like the people in this chapter.

I am confident that you will be excited with the results. Soon, in spite of any failures or hesitancies of the past, you will be sharing Christ more effectively.

Soon, you will be giving the eternal gift.

SUCCESS IN WITNESSING

FAILURE. FEAR of it can be one of the biggest cripplers of a faithful witness, for none of us likes to be "turned down." We tend to take it personally, regarding a rejection of our message as a rejection of our person. It hurts to be turned down.

It hurts even more when we've reached out in genuine love and we see the person refuse the greatest Gift ever offered to mankind, God's Son. Compassion for the lost does not come without tears.

But one of the liberating facts of the Christian life is that God does not ask anything of us that His Son has not already gone through Himself. Jesus Christ, to whom crowds walked miles for teaching and healing, saw His message rejected by many. Unlike us, however, Jesus did not grieve because His ego had been hurt. He grieved because people rejected the Giver of life and the gift of eternal life.

SHARING CHRIST

Did Jesus "Fail" in His Witnessing?

Our Lord's ministry raises some interesting questions: Did He "fail" in His witnessing? Did He fail when the rich young ruler walked away from Him, refusing to give God first place in his life? Did He fail because Judas Iscariot never received Him as his Messiah? Did He fail because a thief crucified with Him refused to acknowledge His lordship? Was He a failure because many in the throngs around Him didn't trust in Him?

Our Lord answered these questions in His prayer to His heavenly Father at the end of His earthly ministry: "I brought glory to you here on earth by doing *everything* you told me to" (John 17:4, emphasis added).

> *Our heavenly Father's command is not to "convert everyone." Jesus did not, and neither can we.*

Despite rejection, or what we might call "failures," our Lord Jesus Christ knew His mission was near completion. He had obeyed His Father's commission. He had brought the message, and was about to complete it with His death and resurrection. While He grieved over those who had rejected Him, He had not failed. He had done "everything" God had given Him to do.

Success in Witnessing

All He Asks Is That We Obey

Our heavenly Father asks no more of us than this: that we obey His command to "go and preach the gospel to every creature." His command is not to "convert everyone." Jesus did not, and neither can we. But we can obey; we can spread the message to all who will listen and trust God for the results.

The ministry of Jesus Christ modeled for us a liberating truth about our witnessing efforts:

> *Success in witnessing is simply taking the initiative to share Christ in the power of the Holy Spirit, and leaving the results to God.*

Jesus never failed in His ministry. He accomplished all that His Father had commissioned Him to do. Likewise, we do not fail if we obey what God wants us to do, motivated by genuine love and compassion.

We fail in witnessing only if we disobey God's command to share His love in the power of the Holy Spirit:

> *Failure in witnessing = failing to witness.*

Had I not learned this truth, I would have been confused and discouraged if someone to whom I had witnessed rejected my message.

SHARING CHRIST

If Christ's example is reliable, the task at hand is not to get results. That may or may not happen. The task to which God has called me is to obey Him and share Christ as effectively and lovingly as I know how.

No-Fail Witnessing

When you obey God, motivated by love, you cannot fail. Your message might be accepted or rejected, but when you share Christ in obedience to God's command and the Holy Spirit's leading, you *succeed* in witnessing, no matter what the immediate result. Again,

> *Success in witnessing is simply taking the initiative to share Christ in the power of the Holy Spirit, and leaving the results to God.*

Read that statement out loud. Memorize it. Whenever the fear of failure begins to immobilize you from obeying God in witnessing, repeat this statement to yourself: Success in witnessing is simply sharing Christ in the power of the Holy Spirit, and leaving the results to God.

This is not to be interpreted as advocating a "hit-and-run" approach to witnessing and ministry, without conscientious follow-up to help new believers get into God's Word and grow in their faith. We firmly believe in the importance of a new Christian getting involved in: 1) a church where our Lord is honored and the Word of God is proclaimed; and 2) systematic training in assurance of salvation, prayer, Bible study, fellowship with others, and Christian growth.

Removing the Burden of "Results"

This definition of successful witnessing is intended to remove from today's frustrated Christian the burden of results. To the faithful witness, there will come many joyous experiences of leading others to Christ. In most countries and cultures, we find that between 25 and 50 percent of those who hear the gospel (when presented by properly trained, Spirit-filled believers) receive Christ as a result. But if these positive numbers are true, then between 50 and 75 percent will say no, at least upon first hearing.

Do the noes constitute failure? Go back to the definitions of success and failure in witnessing. Repeat them aloud. Do these percentages justify our not sharing Christ, because we might hit a streak of noes?

Once I was at Wheaton College in Wheaton,

SHARING CHRIST

Illinois, holding a Lay Institute for Evangelism where we gave training in how to share the gospel. Part of the institute consisted of an afternoon of actual witnessing, door-to-door.

A good friend of mine, a professor at the college, came up to me and said, "I want to go with you, Bill. You're the professional."

"Look," I replied, "there are no professionals. Unless God works in the hearts of men, nothing happens. He only asks us to be obedient and proclaim the message."

My friend thought that since I had taught many Christians how to witness more effectively, perhaps some of the "magic" would rub off on him. And I don't know why the Lord allowed it, but that day was absolutely the worst witnessing experience I've ever had. We were almost bodily thrown out of one house. Another listener reacted very angrily. We didn't see one single person who was interested in even talking with us. We hit an incredible, unexplainable streak of noes all afternoon.

In almost forty years of sharing my faith, I can count on the fingers of one hand the number of hostile rejections that I recall. But a good portion of them seemed to hit all at once on that day!

But, if anything good came of it, the experience made my friend feel better. Maybe God wanted to encourage him by illustrating that even Bill Bright—the supposed "professional" at witnessing—didn't have any power to lead anyone to the Lord unless God Himself did it.

What Christ Taught About Failure

For those who question whether we should even try, considering the chance that a number of listeners will say no, there is assurance for us in the Parable of the Sower. Here, Christ illustrated the varied effectiveness of His message:

> *A farmer was sowing grain in his fields. As he scattered the seed across the ground, some fell beside a path, and the birds came and ate it. And some fell on rocky soil where there was little depth of earth; the plants sprang up quickly enough in the shallow soil, but the hot sun soon scorched them and they withered and died, for they had so little root. Other seeds fell among thorns, and the thorns choked out the tender blades. But some fell on good soil, and produced a crop that was thirty, sixty, and even a hundred times as much as he had planted (Matthew 13:3–8).*

SHARING CHRIST

There are four types of listeners, Christ taught. And only one of the four will take the message (the seed) and put it to work in his life.

The good ground represents the heart of a man who listens to the message and understands it and goes out and brings thirty, sixty, or even a hundred others into the Kingdom (Matthew 13:23).

The other three listeners (types of soil) will squander the message or reject it outright. Jesus Christ Himself recognized that, and though His compassion drove Him to love and long for every human soul, He knew that man would exercise his God-given power of free choice both for and against Him. And man continues to do so today.

We Just Never Know...

So there will be noes. However, we should always presuppose a positive response, since the world is hungrier now for the gospel than ever before. Indeed, the fields are white unto harvest. But when the noes come, we shouldn't be surprised or discouraged.

And we just never know, really, where the noes will lead.

Success in Witnessing

In 1976, Tom and Dorrine, a married couple from Washington, D.C., went witnessing from their church as part of the "I found it!" Here's Life, America campaign. They visited a home where a man and woman, who were living together unmarried, were so loaded on drugs that they couldn't carry on a conversation.

So Tom and Dorrine left a *Four Spiritual Laws* gospel booklet on the coffee table, and suggested that when the couple felt like it they could read the booklet. Tom and Dorrine had received their no, unspoken yet unmistakable.

Two weeks later, the woman came across the booklet and began to read. Its simple gospel presentation convicted her, and she knelt in her living room and received Jesus Christ into her life. Then she gave it to the man she'd been living with, and after several days he pulled out the booklet, read it, and accepted the Lord.

Several weeks passed, and this couple listened to Christian programs on radio and TV. As they heard more of God's Word, they wanted to attend church, and one Sunday they entered the church down the block. It was the same church from which my friends had gone witnessing.

When the pastor gave the invitation, the couple went forward to declare their new faith in God and to be baptized. They ceased living together as singles, but soon were married. Five years later, they had grown so much in their walk with the Lord that he was asked to be a deacon in the church and she was active in several ministries.

When Tom and Dorrine left the haze of this couple's drug-filled living room that day, they must have thought, *Boy, what a waste of time!*

But because of that initial contact, made out of obedience to a God who says, "Go and preach the gospel," God turned this couple's no into a yes and brought two new dedicated believers into His kingdom.

There really is no wasted witness.

The Long Letter

Another no that stands out in my memory is a long letter I wrote to a nationally known sales consultant. I had met him at a conference where he was the featured speaker, and we struck up a conversation and enjoyed a good visit together.

I did share Christ with him, and he seemed interested but was noncommittal. "Why don't you drop me a line with some more information?" he said as we parted company.

Success in Witnessing

I went back to my office and thought and prayed hard about what I would write him. Over the next several days, I felt the Lord guiding me as I pulled together the key Scriptures and concepts of the plan of salvation into a letter to my new friend. I made a copy, mailed him the original, and prayed that God would use my effort in this man's life.

To my knowledge, this gentleman never did receive Christ into his life. He gave me an implied no. But God was working in ways I never would have imagined.

As some trusted friends and I reviewed what I had written in the letter, they suggested that I print it in quantity, under a fictitious salutation, as a witnessing tool. I addressed the letter to a Dr. Van Dusen (I thought he sounded like an intriguing sort) and we printed several thousand copies. Over the years, millions of copies of the "Van Dusen letter" have been printed to meet the demand of our staff, Christian businessmen, and other laypeople who have used it to lead thousands of men and women to the Lord.

God turned this couple's no into a yes and brought two new dedicated believers into His kingdom.

SHARING CHRIST

The Phone Call

One evening during our family dinner time, I received a long-distance phone call. The woman on the other end of the line told me of a printed letter to a "Dr. Van Dusen" which she had found in the seat of a commercial airliner.

"Are you the Bill Bright who wrote this letter?" she asked. She proceeded to ask me some questions, then said, "I would like to become a Christian. Can you help me?"

What a thrill it was to lead this sincere woman in prayer over the phone as she received Christ as her Savior and Lord. But it didn't stop there.

In the family room with her were five other family members and friends. Each of them had read the Van Dusen letter, and they had discussed it together. One by one, each of them came to the phone and, after some questions and discussion, received Christ.

There really is no wasted witness.

We fail in witnessing only if we fail to witness.

Success in witnessing is simply sharing Christ in the power of the Holy Spirit, and leaving the results to God.

THE LOVE OF CHRIST COMPELS US

HAVE YOU EVER felt hesitant to share the gospel because you thought the other person simply would not be interested?

Have you ever sensed the Lord leading you to witness to someone, but you heard a small voice telling you, *You'll only start an argument*?

Or have you been slow to share your faith because you didn't feel you had the gift of evangelism, and witnessing is better left to those with "the gift"?

These are emotions every Christian has felt at one time or another. I certainly have struggled with them. However, during almost sixty years of sharing Christ and helping to train millions of others to do the same, I have been unable to find any biblical rationale to justify those reasons for not witnessing. In fact, from my personal experiences and study of God's Word, five key concepts have been made clear to me—concepts that impact the life of every Christian.

SHARING CHRIST

1. Christ has given a clear commission to every Christian.

Christ commands us to love. True love motivates us to share Christ with others. Paul writes, "For Christ's love compels us, because we are convinced that one died for all, and therefore all died...We are therefore Christ's ambassadors, as though God were making his appeal through us. We implore you on Christ's behalf: Be reconciled to God" (2 Corinthians 5:14,20, NIV).

Jesus Christ was more direct in His last command to His followers: "You are to go into all the world and preach the Good News to everyone, everywhere" (Mark 16:15). This command, which the church calls the Great Commission, was not intended merely for the eleven remaining disciples, or just for the apostles or for those in present times who may have been given the gift of evangelism.

The Great Commission is the duty of every man, woman, and child who confesses Christ as Lord.

This command is the duty of every man, woman, and child who confesses Christ as Lord. We cannot pick and choose which commands of our Lord we will follow. As Harold Lindsell wrote in

The Love of Christ Compels Us

The Lindsell Study Bible, "The evangelization of the whole world is the church's primary mission."

2. Men and women are lost without Jesus Christ.

Jesus said, "I am the way, the truth, and the life. No one comes to the Father except through Me" (John 14:6, NKJ). God's Word reminds us, "There is salvation in no one else! Under all heaven there is no other name for men to call upon to save them" (Acts 4:12).

When I spoke to several hundred students at an evangelistic event at the University of Minnesota, several of them gathered afterward to ask questions. As I counseled them, I noticed an angry young student from India impatiently pacing back and forth.

When I finally was able to interact with him, he practically exploded at me. "I resent you Christians!" he spat out. "You are narrow-minded, arrogant, and bigoted. I am a Hindu—I believe that Christianity is one way to God, but you Christians are not willing to believe that my religion is one way to God."

"I am sorry if I have offended you," I apologized. "But I must remind you that 'I am the way,

SHARING CHRIST

the truth and the life; no man cometh unto the Father, but by me' was a claim that Jesus Christ made for Himself. What do you think of Jesus?"

He thought for a moment. "I would have to say He is the greatest man who ever lived."

I learned from this young man that he was working toward a double doctorate in physics and chemistry. As we talked, I explained more about the claims Jesus made for Himself, how He died for our sin and was raised from the dead, and how His life demonstrated that He was indeed the Son of God. The young man's anger subsided.

"Now tell me," I said, "do you believe that 'the greatest man who ever lived' would lie about Himself? Or do you believe He was a deluded lunatic who just *thought* He was the only way to God?"

The young scholar realized the logic of John 14:6. His countenance changed, as if sunlight had broken through fierce storm clouds in his heart. "Would you like to receive Christ as your Savior and Lord?" I asked. "Yes, I would," he replied. "I understand it now." What a thrill it was to see this brilliant young scholar invite Jesus into his life.

Men and women are truly lost without Jesus Christ. According to God's Word, He is the only

The Love of Christ Compels Us

way to bridge the gap between man and God. Without Him, people cannot know God, and have no hope of eternal life. Always remember: Christ died for the sins of people of all languages, countries, and cultures.

3. Rather than being "not interested," people are truly hungry for the gospel.

In the early 1960s, I was in charge of the student phase of the Bob Pierce Tokyo crusade. There were approximately 500,000 college students in the city, and I was scheduled along with several Campus Crusade leaders to speak at numerous meetings. I was told that nothing like this had ever taken place in Japan, so I boarded the plane with great excitement at the opportunity to present Jesus Christ to the Japanese student world.

Upon arrival, however, my enthusiasm turned to discouragement. We were briefed by a missionary who had been working in Japan for fifteen years.

"Now, the Japanese are different," he warned. "They don't receive the Lord like Americans do."

He went on to explain that the Japanese would normally spend ten, fifteen, twenty years "seeking God" before receiving Christ. They would spend

SHARING CHRIST

all this time in Bible classes, studying diligently, learning all the proper information about Christianity—making salvation a lifelong quest rather than a decisive commitment.

I went back to my room after the briefing, downcast at the prospect of an unsuccessful evangelistic crusade. *Lord*, I prayed, *do You really want me here? I mean, I have so much to do back in the States, and if people here are not interested, maybe someone else could do what I'm doing.*

As I prayed, I sensed a peace coming over my troubled heart. Pascal's famous statement came to mind: "There is in the heart of each man a God-shaped vacuum, which cannot be filled by any created thing; but only by God the Creator, made known through Jesus Christ." It was as if God was assuring me that the Japanese were like anyone else—hungry for God.

The next morning, I spoke in my first meeting to approximately a thousand students. For one hour, I presented the gospel and told stories to illustrate how people's lives have been changed by the power of the living Christ.

At the end of the hour, I said, "We're going to take a five-minute break. If you would like to receive Christ as your Savior and Lord, remain in

The Love of Christ Compels Us

your seat. The rest of you are free to go without any embarrassment. I'll then explain for another hour how you can be sure Christ is in your life and how you can grow spiritually."

The meeting was over. But nobody left.

So I spoke for another hour, walking the audience point-by-point through the gospel message. "Now," I concluded, "we've seen what the Bible tells us about why we need to receive Jesus Christ as our personal Savior and Lord. And you can invite Christ into your life this morning, through a simple prayer. If these words express the desire of your heart, pray with me silently, sincerely:

"Lord Jesus, I need you. Thank You for dying on the cross for my sins. I open the door of my life and receive You as my Savior and Lord. Thank You for forgiving my sins and giving me eternal life. Take control of the throne of my life. Make me the kind of person You want me to be."

I asked the students to raise their hands if they had prayed that prayer. Almost every hand went up.

I practically ran back to my hotel to see the missionary who had briefed us. "Most of those students accepted the Lord!" I exclaimed.

SHARING CHRIST

"Aw, Bill, they don't want to offend you," my missionary friend said, as gently as one can possibly be when throwing cold water on you. "You see, these people appreciate General MacArthur's benevolent treatment of the Japanese after the war. And since you're an American, they don't want to offend you, so they'll do anything you ask them to do."

Again, my balloon deflated. So the next day I went through a similar procedure, with a new group of approximately a thousand students. I spoke for an hour, then gave a clear invitation for those who wanted to receive Jesus Christ. "Now ladies and gentlemen," I concluded, "I'm told that you are staying in these meetings just because you want to be gracious to me —you don't want to offend me because I am an American. But if you have received Jesus into your life today and you know without a doubt that He is in your life, I want you to come and tell me.

"Don't do this if you're just wanting to be

Can we afford to be selfish with the gospel, when there is overwhelming evidence that the majority of people are hungry for God?

courteous to me. Take my hand and tell me the truth, in your own words. I want to know for sure."

And the line formed. I shook hundreds of hands that morning, but more importantly I had the thrill of looking into the glowing faces of young men and women who had just ended their lifelong search for spiritual truth.

People are indeed hungry for the gospel. Jesus said, "Do you think the work of harvesting will not begin until the summer ends four months from now? Look around you! Vast fields of human souls are ripening all around us, and are ready now for reaping" (John 4:35).

We must assume that the family member, neighbor, coworker, or person we've just met will be interested in the good news we have to tell. He may have just gone through a set of circumstances that has prepared his heart to receive Jesus Christ. God may have been leading him into an awareness of his need for the Savior. Perhaps he has felt especially alone or in need of love and forgiveness.

Can we afford to be selfish with the gospel, when there is overwhelming evidence that the majority of people are hungry for God? As Jesus said, "The fields are ripe for harvest."

SHARING CHRIST

4. We Christians have in our possession the greatest gift available to mankind—the greatest news ever announced.

Christ is risen! We serve a living Savior, who not only lives within us in all His resurrection power, but has assured us of eternal life. He died on the cross in our place for our sin, then rose from the dead. We have direct fellowship with God through Jesus Christ. And this fellowship, this peace, this gift of eternal life, is available to all who receive Him.

Why are we so hesitant to share this good news? Why is it that we so readily discuss our political views or athletic preferences, our gas mileage or utility bills, our children's growing pains or our office gossip, but clam up when it comes to discussing the greatest news ever announced?

If our faith in Christ really means as much to us as it should, then it only follows that our faith should be the number-one message on our lips. People *want* to hear good news. And when you present it properly and with love, you will usually see a positive response.

Several years ago, a group of young Christians were singing Christmas carols in Hollywood and Beverly Hills. They had called to make appointments to sing in several celebrities' homes, and then after singing they left behind a copy of the Van Dusen letter, which I had written about Jesus and how one can know Him personally.

One world-famous actor—well-known for his lead roles in two long-lasting family TV series—was particularly gracious to the carolers, and the next day he called the group leader.

"I've read this letter a dozen times," his voice boomed over the phone. "I've never read anything so wonderful. Could I meet Mr. Bright?"

The group leader gave my office the message, and I called the gentleman.

"Mr. Bright—"

"Please, call me Bill," I interrupted. "I've watched your shows enough to feel like I know you already."

"Bill, I know you must be very busy," he apologized. I could sense a feeling of awkward determination in his voice. "I really must see you. I don't want to impose on you, but would you please take a few minutes and see me?"

We arranged to meet at my home. After unfolding himself from his expensive antique car, he bounded up the steps to greet me with a firm handshake and his familiar smile.

SHARING CHRIST

"I've been reading your letter and it's been very meaningful to me," he began, after we had chatted for a few minutes over iced tea. "I've been a member of the vestry of my church in Beverly Hills for years, but I've never read anything like your letter. I don't know Christ personally, and I want you to help me."

We talked briefly about the content of the letter, but he didn't need convincing. He was ready. We got on our knees at the sofa in the living room, and he prayed the most beautiful, heartwarming prayer for salvation I have ever heard. Then, as we stood, he gave me a bear hug that almost cracked my ribs. He went away as delighted as a child at Christmas.

The Scriptures make the good news so clear:

"To all who received Him, He gave the right to become children of God" (John 1:12).

"God so loved the world that He gave His only begotten Son, that whoever believes in Him should not perish but have everlasting life" (John 3:16, NKJ).

"He has rescued us out of the darkness and gloom of Satan's kingdom and brought us into the Kingdom of His dear Son, who bought our

The Love of Christ Compels Us

freedom with His blood and forgave us all our sins" (Colossians 1:13,14).

5. The love of Jesus for us, and our love for Him, compels us to share Him with others.

Jesus Christ said, "The one who obeys Me is the one who loves Me" (John 14:21). In other words, He measures our love for Him by the extent and genuineness of our obedience to Him. And as we obey, He promises He will reveal Himself to us: "because he loves Me, My Father will love him; and I will too, and I will reveal Myself to him" (John 14:21, NKJ).

Jesus measures our love for Him by the extent and genuineness of our obedience to Him.

What are we to obey? When it comes to witnessing, we have the specific commandment from Jesus Christ: "You are to go into all the world and preach the Good News to everyone, everywhere" (Mark 16:15). Helping to fulfill Christ's Great Commission is both a duty and a privilege. We share because we love Christ. We share because He loves us. We share because we want to honor and obey Him. We share because He gives us a special love for others.

To emphasize that specific commandment, we

SHARING CHRIST

are called to be obedient to God's daily guidance as He brings us in contact with people from all walks of life. We've all experienced that special feeling, that whisper deep inside prompting us, *Tell this person about Jesus Christ.* But, for one reason or another (fear, rushed schedule, not knowing what to say), we're tempted to neglect the whisper and proceed with "more important things."

We have a ringing command from our Lord to share the gospel, and men and women are lost without Him. Indeed, they are hungry for the good news, and we Christians have in our possession the greatest news ever announced. Our love for the Lord—and His love for us—compels us to obey Him as He leads us into the sharing opportunities of each day.

BARRIERS TO WITNESSING

AS A MINISTRY that specializes in helping train laypeople in effective evangelism, we have made extensive studies of why Christians don't share their faith more readily. We've found that, while some believe "religion should be personal and private," most Christians recognize the biblical imperative for a personal witness. But they allow three barriers to keep them from witnessing.

Barrier 1: Spiritual Lethargy

If you aren't excited about something, chances are you won't tell many people about it. And we find that in the lives of far too many Christians, the excitement of the Christian walk has been dulled by everyday distractions, materialistic pursuits, and unconfessed sin. Like the believers in the church of Ephesus, these men and women have "left their first love" (their total devotion and obedience to Jesus Christ).

SHARING CHRIST

Following one of my lectures on the lordship of Christ, a bright young educator came to see me. His credentials were superb: an earned doctorate, an already successful career, and prospects for even further upward mobility. But something was bothering him.

"I became a Christian several years ago when I was a young boy," he began. "But through the years I gradually took back the control of my life. I am still active in the church. Yet, I'm ashamed to say that I've been more interested in promoting my own business and social position than I have been in serving the Lord and getting to know Him better. I have compromised my business and professional standards, and have not always been honest and ethical in my dealings with others.

"God has shown me that I have wasted many years living selfishly for my own interests. Now I want to help reach the world for Christ."

We prayed together, and rejoiced in his new commitment. Up to that moment he had been living in spiritual lethargy—self-centered, carnal, and with little desire to share the love of Christ with others. Upon his rededication, however, he became a confident, effective witness.

If you have felt spiritually dry or defeated, it

Barriers to Witnessing

is possible that you have "left your first love." Perhaps you've allowed the hectic pace of life to distract you from quality times of prayer and meditation on God's Word. Perhaps you have allowed society's pervasive message of humanism and self-gratification to lure you toward "the good life"—and away from the best life. Perhaps these and other offenses toward God have festered into unconfessed sin.

In Psalm 66:18 we read, "If I regard iniquity in my heart, the Lord will not hear me" (KJV). Unconfessed sin short-circuits our fellowship with God and makes us like those Christians Paul describes in 1 Corinthians 3:1–3:

> *And I, brethren, could not speak to you as to spiritual people but as to carnal, as to babes in Christ...for you are still carnal. For where there are envy, strife, and divisions among you, are you not carnal and behaving like mere men? (NASB)*

The carnal Christian described by Paul does not feel constrained to share Christ because his attention is focused on himself rather than on others. He has allowed love of things, love of distractions, and unconfessed sin to take his eyes off

SHARING CHRIST

Christ. He has left his first love.

If these symptoms describe your spiritual life, you can restore your first love—your intimacy and joy in the Savior—by taking two important steps.

First, keep Christ "on the throne." To understand your life, picture a large throne. This represents your "control center," or your will. When you received Christ as Savior and Lord, you invited Him into your life and onto the throne—you deliberately surrendered the control and guidance of your life to Him.

However, when you yield to temptation and sin, you take back control of that throne. Christ is still in your life, but He is no longer on the throne. God created you with free will, and He wants you to choose freely whether you obey or disobey Him.

Paul identified this problem when he wrote:

> *I don't understand myself at all, for I really want to do what is right, but I can't. I do what I don't want to—what I hate...But I can't help myself because I'm no longer doing it. It is sin inside me that is stronger than I am that makes me do these evil things.*
>
> *I know I am rotten through and through so far as my old sinful nature is concerned. No mat-*

Barriers to Witnessing

ter which way I turn I can't make myself do right. I want to but I can't (Romans 7:15–18).

Second, practice "Spiritual Breathing." Spiritual Breathing is simply the act of again surrendering to God the control of the throne of your life, by confessing sin and accepting His loving forgiveness. This concept is one of the most vital truths of God's Word. It is the key to daily victory over the constant pull of sin in your life.

Just as we exhale and inhale physically, so we can exhale and inhale spiritually. We "exhale" when we confess our sins, and we "inhale" when we appropriate the cleansing, control, and power of God's Holy Spirit.

- *Exhale by confessing any known sin in your life.* Wait quietly before God. Ask Him to reveal to you, through His Holy Spirit, any areas in your life that are not right.

    As the Holy Spirit brings these to mind, agree with God in prayer that you have sinned, and appropriate His forgiveness, promised in 1 John 1:9: "If we confess our sins, He is faithful and just to forgive us our sins and to cleanse us from all unrighteousness" (NKJ).

    To help you better understand the importance of confession, the original meaning of the word *confess* means "to agree with." As you agree with God concerning sin in your life, you are saying at least three things to Him: 1) "God, I agree with You that these things I'm doing [list them] are wrong"; 2) "I agree with You that Christ died on the cross for these sins"; and 3) "I repent—I consciously turn my mind and heart from my sins and, as an act of my will, I turn my actions toward obedience to You."

- *Inhale by being filled with God's Holy Spirit.* Being filled with the Spirit is the secret of living the Christian life. It simply means allowing Christ, through His Holy Spirit, to empower and guide you moment by moment, day by day.

  The same Holy Spirit who empowered the disciples at Pentecost to "turn the world upside down" is available to each of us today. We are commanded in Ephesians 5:18 to be filled with (controlled, directed, guided by) the Spirit. On the authority of God's promise that He will answer us if we pray according to His will (1 John 5:14,15), and since it is His will that we

Barriers to Witnessing

be filled with His Spirit, you can ask God right now, in faith, and He will fill you with the Holy Spirit.

After learning the concept of Spiritual Breathing at our training conferences, thousands of people have told us that this one simple truth has completely changed their walk with the Lord. For example, Jeff had been a Christian since childhood, but he had felt frustrated with his "roller coaster" commitment to Christ. When he learned how to be filled with the Spirit and keep God on the throne of his life through Spiritual Breathing, he consciously began telling the Lord, "I give you control of the throne of my life. Guide me, and give me wisdom and strength today to act, talk, and think the way You want me to." From a life of constant defeat, he began to live in the victory and joy of our risen Lord.

The Holy Spirit will convict you when you've sinned, nudge you to extend a caring hand to a neighbor, fill you with a reservoir of love to give to others, and urge you to share your faith with the people around you. Your obedience to His daily prompting will keep you from ever wanting to leave your first love.

SHARING CHRIST

Barrier 2: Believing the Enemy's "Lines"

"We do not wrestle against flesh and blood, but against principalities, against powers, against the rulers of the darkness of this age," Paul tells us (Ephesians 6:12, NKJ).

There is a definite spiritual battle raging. The Bible says that "God has rescued us out of the darkness and gloom of Satan's kingdom" (Colossians 1:13). Every Christian was once a member of that kingdom, and those nonbelievers with whom we share Christ are still members of Satan's kingdom. It's not a pleasant thought, but nonbelievers are there either by choice, ignorance, or default, and Satan is doing everything he can to retain his control.

So as you sense God leading you to tell someone about Jesus, Satan's agents go to work. You may even hear some very believable "lines" from his direction that are intended to make you think twice, turn heel, and abandon your good intentions. Following are several examples.

"Mind your own business. You don't have any right to force your views on someone else."

If you hear this line, ask yourself, "Where would

Barriers to Witnessing

I be today if the person who introduced me to Christ had 'minded his own business'?"

When we share Christ in a gentle spirit of love, we aren't "forcing" our views on anyone. We speak gently and lovingly; the hearer is free to listen, change the subject, or move away.

"You're going to offend this person. Don't say anything."

If someone you know were dying of cancer and you knew the cure for the disease, would you avoid telling him about the cure because you might offend him?

Of course not. You would gladly share the good news that his cancer can be cured. Why should we be any less enthusiastic about sharing the Ultimate Cure over the ultimate disease?

"He'll think you're a fanatic."

Yes, he might. But then again, he might be the one person whom God has specially prepared for you on this day. Not everyone will accept the gospel—even Jesus encountered men and women who rejected His message. Our role is not to convert, but to obey. We can dislodge the "fanatic" stereotype with a confident, loving, logical presen-

SHARING CHRIST

tation of the claims of Christ, shared in the power of the Holy Spirit.

"Distractions, interruptions. Interruptions, distractions."

The phone rings. Someone else enters the room. A baby cries for attention. Someone turns on the television. When you set out to raid Satan's kingdom, you have to believe he will counterattack. He can engineer circumstances to place all kinds of obstacles between you and the person with whom you're sharing.

Whenever I find myself in such a situation, I pray silently, even as we're talking, that God would bind Satan and allow my friend to hear the message and make a free choice. It's definitely a spiritual battle, but you can be assured that if Satan is causing problems, he's worried. You must be doing something right.

"The person will say no, and I'll be embarrassed."

We are often guilty of presenting the gospel with an attitude that says, "Uh...you wouldn't want to receive the greatest Gift available to mankind, would you?" We don't realize how many people are really ready to accept Christ, if only someone would show them how. Our philosophy of witnessing should not be, "I'm sure he'll say no to Jesus," but rather, "Who could say no to Jesus?" We should always presuppose a positive response.

Barrier 3: Lack of Practical "Know-How"

"What do I say?"

"What Scripture verses do I use?"

"How do I begin a conversation about Jesus?"

"How should I respond to questions or arguments?"

"How can I be sure he understands?"

"How do I encourage a decision?"

As a result of thousands of surveys, we have found that the vast majority of Christians today not only believe they *should* share their faith, they really *want* to share their faith. Many Christians hear repeated messages from the pulpit that they should be "taking Christ to the marketplace" but they don't receive the practical, hands-on training that will ease their fears and help them witness effectively. The result is a guilt trip: They know they should, but they hesitate because they don't know how.

SHARING CHRIST

I am encouraged as I see more and more pastors providing evangelism training to their laypeople. There are many excellent training programs available to churches today. To become effective, you don't need a seminary degree or endless drills that prepare you for every conceivable situation. Within a couple of hours, you can learn a method of sharing Christ that has proven effective for millions of Christians around the world.

Thousands of pastors have taken this training, as have students and laypeople, who in turn have used it to witness to their loved ones, friends, neighbors, and acquaintances. We have hundreds of stories on file of people who received Christ through this presentation, then went out and led someone else to the Lord within forty-eight hours. It's simple, effective, and transferable.

We don't claim that it's the only way to share the gospel, or even the best way; but it is one method that works. This book can be your training ground to help you gain the practical know-how of sharing your faith with confidence.

PREPARATION FOR WITNESSING

SHE WAS IN her mid-fifties, and as she approached me following a lecture, her eyes were red from weeping. "Our son is almost thirty," she began, her voice trembling, "and he is still living a rebellious life. I don't think he's a Christian and I don't know how to get through to him."

This woman's story was like hundreds I hear every year from concerned fellow believers: a family member, a neighbor, a friend, or a coworker needs Christ. The concerned believer has been praying for that person—sometimes for years—without an apparent answer to the prayers.

I'm sure that must have been the feeling my saintly mother had as she prayed for her children and for my dear father. Mother and Dad were married thirty years before Dad received Christ. Their love for each other was strong, but Dad's indifference to the Lord must have caused my mother to shed many tears. But she kept praying—for him, and for my brothers and sisters and me—

SHARING CHRIST

until finally, thirty years later, her prayers began to see results and eventually our entire family placed their faith in our Lord.

I have prayed intensively for hundreds of others over the years and, while many have received Christ, others still have not. So I can readily identify with the concerned believer whose heart aches for the salvation of a friend or loved one. From my personal experience and study of God's Word, I can assure you that the key starting point in bringing a loved one to Christ is prayer.

Just as Jesus prayed that the Holy Spirit would do a work in the lives of His disciples, so we can pray that the Holy Spirit will convict a nonbeliever and give him a strong desire for the ways of God. God's Word assures us that the Lord is "not willing that any should perish but that all should come to repentance" (2 Peter 3:9, NKJ). God desires the soul of your loved one, friend, or neighbor even more than you do.

Sometimes, however, in His mysterious, sovereign timing, He chooses to wait for the prayers of a concerned believer to unleash the Holy Spirit in that person's life. As someone has said, "Prayer is not conquering God's reluctance but laying hold of God's willingness."

Preparation for Witnessing

How to Pray for Your Friends and Loved Ones

God commands us to pray without ceasing and to devote ourselves to prayer (1 Thessalonians 5:17 and Colossians 4:2). Prayer is foundational to our spiritual vitality and to our ongoing witness for Christ. As Louis Evans, Jr., wrote, "The man who kneels to God can stand up to anything."

Make prayer a daily foundation of your faith in Jesus Christ. Do not make the mistake of praying simply for your own personal intimacy with the Savior, or for the endless lists of "things" for which we always ask God. We must pray daily for the souls of our friends and loved ones, asking God what role He would have us play in their exposure to His plan for their lives.

Likewise, we must be in a constant attitude of prayer for those we might encounter on a casual basis, realizing that God wants us to proclaim the good news to all who will listen. As we pray for the Holy Spirit's wisdom and power, and for the open minds and hearts of the listeners, God will truly bless our efforts to share with them about His forgiveness.

As you pray for your friends, loved ones, co-workers, and neighbors:

SHARING CHRIST

1. Be sure you are a Christian, and that there is no unconfessed sin in your life.

Have you actually received Jesus Christ as your own personal Savior and Lord? This, of course, is the first step. By inviting Him to take control of your life, you can be assured that He is indeed in your life and that you have moved from the kingdom of darkness to the kingdom of light.

Then, since God does not hear the prayer of a sinful heart, it is vital that you apply the principles of Spiritual Breathing moment by moment, day by day. Refer to Chapter 4 to be sure you understand how to "exhale the impure" (confess sin) and "inhale the pure" (appropriate God's promised forgiveness and cleansing). As you breathe spiritually, fellowship with God is restored, and your prayers will be heard.

2. Pray in faith, believing God will do the work you're asking Him to do.

Are you eager to see your friends and loved ones receive Christ? Then begin today to pray in faith.

> *Successful praying is simply asking God to work according to His promised will, and leaving the results to Him.*

Preparation for Witnessing

Make a list of all for whom you're praying. Keep a prayer journal and make notes of special things that happen to them as time passes. Ask God for the salvation of each friend and loved one, and realize the liberating truth that God loves them even more than you do. Pray regularly, thanking God in faith that He is at work drawing them to Himself.

3. Be sure your lifestyle reflects Jesus Christ.

"How can we be sure that we belong to him?" the apostle John asks. "By looking within ourselves: are we really trying to do what he wants us to? Someone may say, 'I am a Christian; I am on my way to heaven; I belong to Christ.' But if he doesn't do what Christ tells him to, he is a liar" (1 John 2:3,4).

If the Holy Spirit points out areas where your words, actions, or attitudes are inconsistent with your walk with the Lord, ask God to change those negative patterns. "Walk in the Spirit" by allowing the Spirit of the Lord to infuse you with the attributes of Jesus Christ.

Ask God to make you loving, positive, honest, and caring in all aspects of your life. Ask Him to

SHARING CHRIST

remind you quickly when you slip into a behavioral pattern that presents a negative witness.

4. Share Christ verbally as opportunities arise.

Someone has said, "Prayer is not an argument with God to persuade Him to move things our way, but an exercise by which we are enabled by His Spirit to move ourselves His way." In praying for the salvation of friends and loved ones, this quite often is the case. Our prayer for others prompts and enables us to give verbal witness to that very person, if only we obey God's prompting.

Could it be that God has not yet answered your prayer because you have not been willing to be the bearer of His message? You have in your possession the most joyful news ever announced. You have been praying urgently for this person. Is there any scriptural reason why you shouldn't make the good news clear to your friend or loved one?

The next time you're alone with this person, consider it a divine appointment—an opportunity God has brought specifically to you to share the gospel with confidence. Remember: Success in witnessing is simply taking the initiative to share

Preparation for Witnessing

Christ in the power of the Holy Spirit, and leaving the results to God.

5. Trust in God's timing.

Your friend or loved one may surprise you and eagerly accept Christ as Savior upon first hearing the gospel. If the person does not respond at the first opportunity, continue to pray, thanking God in faith that He will answer according to His expressed will. Continue fellowship with the person, to show your unconditional love. Conscientiously model the positive, victorious Christian life through your attitudes, actions, and words. As the Lord leads you, talk about Jesus again in your conversations, without hesitancy or embarrassment.

Conscientiously model the positive, victorious Christian life through your attitudes, actions, and words.

You have planted the seed. If it takes root in a fertile heart, God will harvest that seed in His sovereign timing. He may use you, He may use someone else, or He may bring your loved one to Himself in a special way. So keep praying, loving, and trusting.

SHARING CHRIST

How to Guide a Conversation Toward Jesus

"I had a great opportunity to talk with someone about Christ today," a sharp young woman once told me, "but I just couldn't think of a way to begin. I felt very awkward. How do you guide a conversation toward Jesus in a way that's natural and doesn't seem contrived?"

Some folks practically shout "Repent!" as if from some street corner in the inner city. Others inch their way ever so cautiously toward spiritual things—so cautiously, in fact, that the conversation never does get around to the Lord Jesus.

I'm not personally comfortable with the first approach. And I know from experience that the second can get so easily sidetracked that the gospel usually loses out to the weather, football, or stories of Johnny's latest escapades at school.

So there needs to be a happy medium—a means of turning a conversation toward Christ that is natural and sensitive, yet which helps the person you're talking with face his need for the Savior. Let's examine effective ways to lead into a gospel presentation.

Basically, the person you're talking with falls into one of two categories: 1) a loved one, friend,

Preparation for Witnessing

neighbor, or coworker, or 2) a casual encounter—someone next to you on a bus or plane, a waitress or cab driver, the person seated next to you at a concert or seminar, or a business contact.

Friendship Evangelism vs. Initiative Evangelism

For the person with whom you're in frequent contact, your approach should generally be less direct. It's important to take the time to build a relationship of friendship and trust, to show by word and deed that you love and care about the person. This approach has been called "friendship evangelism" by some, and it does have its place. Especially important among family members, but also recommended for other close relationships, friendship evangelism urges a "go slow" approach that is intended to virtually love the non-Christian into God's kingdom.

But with its strengths also come two glaring weaknesses. First, many Christians mistakenly subscribe to the friendship evangelism philosophy to the extent that they rarely share the gospel with another because "our relationship isn't quite strong enough yet." Then, when they feel the relationship finally is strong, they are afraid to say anything that might spoil the friendship. To justify this approach, or non-approach, they decide they'll "wait for the nonbeliever to ask me about my personal faith," and try to simply model Christianity through their nonverbal witness. As a result, the gospel often falls by the wayside.

The second weakness of the friendship evangelism philosophy is that Christians can use it as an excuse to never share their faith. Some Christian authors have written that "initiative evangelism" (sharing Christ with casual encounters, door-to-door canvassing, etc.) will almost invariably turn off the non-Christian because it cannot present Jesus Christ from a basis of friendship and relational trust.

Yet, we see initiative evangelism modeled for us throughout Scripture. Jesus had only a few moments with the Samaritan woman He met at the well, but He took the initiative to talk to her about Living Water. In Philip's brief encounter with the Ethiopian eunuch, he led the stranger to Christ. Paul wrote, "Everywhere we go we talk about Christ to all who will listen" (Colossians 1:28).

As I have suggested, I believe there is a place for friendship evangelism, and I would be wrong to say that the philosophy of friendship evangelism

Preparation for Witnessing

is unscriptural. Likewise, those who hold that it is the only way to share Christ, and that initiative evangelism is unscriptural or ineffective, are just as wrong. A careful reading of the New Testament makes it emphatically clear that initiative evangelism is the intent of our Lord when He commands us to "go into all the world, and preach the gospel to every creature."

Both approaches have their proper place in the task of spreading the gospel. But I am convinced that if I were to err in sharing Christ, the Lord would prefer that I err on the side of taking initiative than in not sharing Him at all.

"LETUS": Five Important Steps

Let's look at five important steps for guiding a conversation toward Jesus. These will prove helpful whether you're sharing with a close acquaintance or a casual encounter. To help you remember them, utilize the acrostic LETUS.

L ove
E stablish rapport
T alk about Jesus
U se stories (if time allows)
S equence of questions

SHARING CHRIST

Love. Your motivation should be love, and the other person should see it in your eyes and facial expressions, hear it in your voice, and witness it in your attitudes and actions. If he senses that you're speaking to him out of obligation or to attain a spiritual trophy, he'll turn cold in a hurry. Paul wrote, "Let love be without hypocrisy" (Romans 12:9, NKJ).

To help us obey that command, God promises in 1 John 5:14,15 that if we ask anything according to His will, He will hear and answer us. So, to be sure you are reaching out in genuine love, ask God for His love to flow through you.

The first listed fruit of the Spirit is love (Galatians 5:22). You can trust that as God controls you through His Holy Spirit, He will fill you with love for others. And you can communicate that love by taking sincere interest in the other person through friendly conversation, eye contact, a pleasant facial expression, and questions to keep the conversation going.

Establish rapport. Take the time to establish rapport. In some situations, it might be just a few moments—one brief comment or two to express friendliness. Other times, such as on an airplane or with an acquaintance, you may want to take more

Preparation for Witnessing

time to ask the other person about his vocation, interests, etc.

In training home visitation teams, we usually advise a visit of five minutes at the most before leading in to the gospel, since team members are unexpected guests in the person's home. Be sensitive to the surroundings and to the other person's time constraints.

Talk about Jesus. A common mistake among Christians who are beginning to share their faith is that they allow conversations to become sidetracked. It is generally best not to talk about religions, denominations, churches, and personalities. Many people have bitter remembrances—real or imagined—from their past about these peripheral issues. But if you stay focused on the person of Jesus Christ, your listener can't help but be attracted to Him.

A taxi driver in Australia said to me, "I gave up all religion in World War II. I want nothing to do with a God who allows people to kill each other."

"Wait a minute," I objected. "You are accusing God of something for which man is responsible. It's the evil in man—his sin—that causes him to hate and steal and kill."

I explained to him the difference between re-

SHARING CHRIST

ligion, which is man's search for God, and Christianity, which is God's revelation of Himself to man through Jesus Christ. As I focused on Jesus, the cab driver's whole attitude changed. After we reached our destination, he prayed with me, asking Christ to come into his life.

Use stories (if time allows). The word "witness" literally means to give testimony of facts or events. In other words, to tell the true story of how Christ has changed your life, and the lives of others.

The New Testament Christians witnessed by telling stories of how Jesus died and rose from the dead, how He changed their lives, and what He offered to everyone who would receive Him. Paul told of his dramatic conversion experience. Their witness through stories not only caught the attention of the listeners, but showed them vividly how they, too, could commit themselves to the Lord.

One of the most effective ways we've found to lead in to a discussion of the gospel is a sequence of directed questions.

Stories are among the most effective methods of teaching. Think back to the most recent sermon you heard. Which do you remember best: the con-

Preparation for Witnessing

cept upon concept of the message, or the stories the pastor told to illustrate those concepts?

At Campus Crusade for Christ, we teach each of our new staff, and everyone who goes through our training conferences, to write out, polish, and memorize a three-minute testimony. It should cover three basic points: 1) what your life was like before you received Christ; 2) how you received Christ; and 3) what your life is like since you received Christ. We encourage everyone to be as specific as possible, humorous if appropriate, and very clear when explaining how they invited Christ into their lives (so that if the listener were to have no other opportunity, he would know from the three-minute testimony how he can receive Christ as Savior).

Let me strongly encourage you to write and memorize your own three-minute testimony. Practice delivering it conversationally, perhaps with a friend. You'll be surprised how often it will come in handy in speaking engagements and witnessing opportunities—and at how effective it can be in helping you move from casual conversation to the actual gospel.

Sequence of questions. One of the most effective ways we've found to lead in to a discussion of the

SHARING CHRIST

gospel is a sequence of directed questions. They can be used whether you have just a few minutes with someone or you've known that person for a lifetime.

The first group of questions I'll share with you is helpful to use after a non-Christian has attended a Christian event (church service, lecture, concert, seminar) or if you have given the nonbeliever a Christian book, magazine, or tape. After the event, or after the person has had a chance to read or listen to what you gave him, ask:

1. "What did you think of the concert?" (church service, book, etc.)

2. "Did it make sense to you?"

3. "Have you made the wonderful discovery of knowing Christ personally?"

4. "You'd like to, wouldn't you?" Or, "Would you like to?"

Listen intently to the person's answer to each question, then ask the next one in the sequence. You'll see that each subsequent question is appropriate to ask no matter what answer was given to the preceding question. The fourth question provides a natural lead-in to the gospel presentation.

Preparation for Witnessing

We have taught hundreds of thousands, if not millions, of Christian high school and college students and laypeople to approach their friends with these questions following a Christian concert, drama series, or other event. For example, after a performance by André Kole, a Christian illusionist, you might see dozens of clusters of young people throughout the auditorium as Christian students take the initiative to ask others, "What did you think of the performance? Did his comments about Jesus Christ make sense to you? Have you made the discovery of knowing Christ personally? Would you like to?"

In the majority of cases, the person who answers "no" or "I'm not sure" to the third question will say "yes" or "perhaps" to the fourth. And the door is open for the gospel.

six
SHARING THE GOOD NEWS

IN THE FIRST chapter, I told you of several Christians who had felt inadequate in sharing Christ with others. After just a few hours of training in how to be filled with the Holy Spirit and how to use the *Four Spiritual Laws* booklet, each of them was able to introduce someone to the Lord.

Jackie led one of her neighbors to Christ, and her husband, Steve, led his mother and Jackie's father to Him.

Al used the presentation in a prison to introduce an inmate to the Savior.

Burt reports seeing "consistent results as others respond to God's love through my witness."

Kathy led her neighbor, Sue, to Christ.

All of these people, and thousands of others like them, are continuing to take the initiative to share Christ in the power of the Holy Spirit, and leaving the results to God. And God is honoring their faithfulness.

Like these fellow believers, you are about to

SHARING CHRIST

discover how easy it can be to utilize the *Four Spiritual Laws* (as well as *Would You Like to Know God Personally?*) in your witnessing opportunities. The principles you'll learn in this chapter are appropriate for either booklet.

Recognizing the Benefits

Over the years, those who have used the *Four Spiritual Laws* presentation have realized several consistent benefits:

- It enables you to be prepared for practically any witnessing situation.

- It gives you confidence because you know what you are going to say and how you're going to say it.

- It makes it possible for you to be brief.

- It can be used to open the conversation. You can simply say, "Have you heard of the *Four Spiritual Laws?*"

- It begins on a positive note: "God loves you."

- It presents the claims of Christ clearly.

- It includes an invitation to receive Christ.

- It offers suggestions for growth.
- It emphasizes the importance of the church.
- It enables you to stay on the subject.
- It gives you something tangible to leave with the person, either to reinforce the commitment he's made or to consider for a later decision.

Preparing to Share

It is important to be prepared for the witnessing opportunities that God brings your way. The following five steps will help your occasions to share Christ go more smoothly.

Pray. As already emphasized, prayer is an essential foundation to successful witnessing. At the beginning of each day, ask God to make you sensitive and obedient to His leading as you interact with friends, loved ones, neighbors, co-workers, and casual encounters. Ask Him to prepare the hearts of those to whom He might lead you and to give you wisdom in sharing His love. In addition, pray silently as you begin to share the gospel, that God would communicate through you in such a way that the hearer can make an intelligent, heartfelt decision.

SHARING CHRIST

Be sure you are controlled by the Holy Spirit. At the start of each day, be sure Christ is "on the throne" of your life. If the Holy Spirit is not in control of your life, your efforts will come from legalism rather than love. Then, as the Holy Spirit makes you aware of sin in your life, breathe spiritually. Exhale the impure (confess any known sin) and inhale the pure (surrender control of your life to Christ, and appropriate the control and power of the Holy Spirit).

Always keep a supply of booklets handy. Keep two or three *Four Spiritual Laws* booklets in your pocket, wallet, or purse. You never know when the opportunity will present itself to use one, or several. Most Christian bookstores stock them, or you can order them directly from New*Life* Publications (see the Resources).

Memorize the Four Spiritual Laws presentation. This isn't a must, as long as you have a booklet to help you. But it's inevitable that opportunities will arise to share the gospel when a booklet isn't available, or when it would be awkward to use one (such as when speaking before a group of three or more).

With just a little worthwhile effort, you can easily memorize the text and verses of the presentation (key verses that every Christian should know). Mark, a layman who decided to memorize the first twelve pages of the booklet, was glad he did. One day while he was having coffee with his boss, the conversation turned toward spiritual values. Mark didn't have any booklets with him, but because he had memorized the presentation he was able to write out the four principles on a napkin, diagrams and all. And there, in the doughnut shop, Mark's boss asked Jesus Christ into his life.

LETUS. Review the LETUS acrostic from Chapter 5. Reach out in *love*. Take time to *establish* rapport. *Talk* about Jesus (keep the conversation focused on Him). *Use* stories from your own experience (your three-minute testimony) if time allows. Utilize a *sequence* of questions to lead into the booklet.

Presenting the Four Spiritual Laws

Now let's look at the important elements of presenting the gospel through the *Four Spiritual Laws*.

Be sensitive to the leading of the Holy Spirit and to the individual's interest. The simplest way to explain the *Four Spiritual Laws* is to read the booklet aloud. However, be careful not to allow the presentation to become mechanical. Remember,

SHARING CHRIST

you are not *preaching to* or even *reading to* the listener; you are *sharing with*. You are introducing the person to the Lord Jesus Christ, and the *Four Spiritual Laws* is simply a communication tool. Continually pray for God's love to be expressed through you.

Hold the booklet so it can be seen clearly. Use a pen or pencil to keep the listener's eye focused on the text.

Stick to the presentation. There is nothing magical about the *Four Spiritual Laws*. But over the years, our staff and the students and laypeople we have trained have learned that it is usually best to share the text just as it is written, word for word without comment. This helps to assure that the essential basics of the gospel are presented and that they don't get lost in peripheral discussion.

Defer most questions, graciously. When questions arise that would change the subject, explain that the majority of questions are answered as you go through the booklet. In most cases, once the listener has seen the full presentation, his questions will be answered. If you're not sure whether his question is answered in the booklet, you can say, "That's an excellent question. Let's talk about it after we've read through the booklet." You'll

Sharing the Good News

find that the questions usually fade in importance as the listener sees the full presentation in its context.

Be sensitive as you share. If there seems to be no response, stop and ask, "Is this making sense?" If the listener is interested but has time constraints, give him the booklet and encourage him to read through it that night. If he says he's not interested at all, give him the booklet and say, "Perhaps there'll come a time when spiritual things *are* of special interest to you—why don't you take this with you so you can study it when that time comes?"

There are times, such as on a noisy airplane, when I simply hand the booklet to a person and ask him to read it and tell me what he thinks. After he has read it, I'll touch on the highlights, then read the fourth law and the suggested prayer word-for-word.

If you're sharing with a small group: Give each person a booklet. Pray with those who are interested in receiving Christ. If only one is interested, talk with him privately after the others have left.

Be confident! Be assured that if you are walking in the Spirit, it is indeed God's will for you to share your faith with this person. You have a di-

SHARING CHRIST

vine appointment. Remember: *Success in witnessing is simply taking the initiative to share Christ in the power of the Holy Spirit, and leaving the results to God.* If you obey, no matter what the results, you cannot fail!

Pulling It All Together

In our training conferences, we pair our conferees to practice one-to-one delivery of the *Four Spiritual Laws* with each other. Let me encourage you to find a friend with whom you can practice, to shake out the initial jitters you might feel as you begin to read through the booklet aloud. Invite the person to be a "friendly listener" at this point, posing no objections or questions. The aim is to get you comfortable with the basic presentation. Next, we are going to look at how to handle some potential questions and smokescreens that might come your way.

How to Handle Hostility, Questions, and Resistance

As you faithfully share Christ with others, you will occasionally encounter hostility, questions, and resistance. Be sensitive to the leading of the Holy Spirit. There is a time to bring an end to a conversation, give the listener something to read, and encourage him to invite Christ into his life when ready.

But you will also find that, in the majority of cases, a listener's initial resistance really signifies that he wants to know more. His questions indicate that he's sincerely interested in clarifying some important points, and any initial hostility is in reality a mask to hide a deep-down cry for help.

General Guidelines

To help you guide the listener through such smokescreens so he can focus on the person of Jesus Christ and make an intelligent decision, let's establish some important general guidelines:

1. Never argue. Remember, your mission is to proclaim the good news, not to win an argument. Let the genuine *agape* love of God pervade your words, your tone of voice, and your facial expressions. Answer questions and ask questions, but do not argue.

2. Don't try to reason within the listener's sphere of expertise. I studied philosophy, but I would have dug quite a hole for myself if I had tried to reason philosophically with some individuals I have encountered. I studied science, but I wouldn't fare

SHARING CHRIST

well if I tried to reason from science with a scientist. So I try to stay focused on the person of Jesus Christ—His love, His death and resurrection, His gift of eternal life.

3. Remember what God has commissioned you to do. Your task is to proclaim; it is God's task to convert. Share the claims of Christ thoroughly. Answer questions calmly, to the best of your ability. Give the listener ample opportunity to respond. In most cases, he will respond favorably. But if he doesn't, you have planted a seed—and you can trust God with the results. Remember:

> *Successful witnessing is simply taking the initiative to share Christ in the power of the Holy Spirit, and leaving the results to God.*

4. Try to get the listener into the Four Spiritual Laws as quickly as possible. Whenever appropriate, use the question or objection as a means to transition into the presentation. Many questions and objections will be resolved in the listener's mind as he sees the full context of the gospel.

5. Appeal to the listener's intellectual integrity. No one wants to be "intellectually dishonest," but this is precisely the error many people make when resisting God's Word—it is the one thing they refuse

Sharing the Good News

to investigate objectively. By appealing to their intellectual integrity, you can help them see that they should indeed give the gospel a fair hearing.

6. If the listener rejects the gospel, always leave him with something to read. Give him the *Four Spiritual Laws* booklet or a Gospel of John, along with a challenge to do the "30-Day Experiment" (explained below). The principle is, literature distribution is the next-best thing to being there. So always give the listener something to take home for further study.

When Questions Might Come

Questions, resistance, and objections typically occur in one of three places during your sharing opportunity:

- During the lead-in conversation, prior to the presentation of the *Four Spiritual Laws*

- During the presentation, particularly regarding the circle diagram on page 9

- Following the reading of the suggested prayer on page 10

If an objection comes up during lead-in conversation, you can deal with it briefly and then

SHARING CHRIST

use it to bridge into the Four Laws presentation. For example, your listener states, "I don't feel that God could love me after the things I've done." You could say, "You know, it's amazing—I've discovered that God loves us in spite of what we've done. In fact, I've come across a little booklet that explains it beautifully; would you like to see what the Bible says about God's love?"

If an objection comes up while you're reading through the booklet, remember to defer the question, graciously, to the end of the presentation. The only exception to this guideline is if the listener is obviously irritated and doesn't want you to continue. If this should happen, apologize: "I'm sorry if I have offended you. Here, why don't you keep the booklet and read through it yourself, when you're ready?"

If questions or objections are raised after you have invited the listener to pray the suggested prayer, *now* is the time to patiently address each question. You have laid the foundation by showing the four biblical principles. If his questions weren't answered by the context of the presentation, try to answer them now. Never push or rush a decision for Christ. When you sense that the listener's questions have been answered, you can gently ask, "Would you like to receive Christ right now?"

The 30-Day Experiment

The person who contends "I don't believe" is usually more of a candidate for the kingdom than one who says, "I don't care." I have found that in many cases, those who say they don't believe in God, the Bible, or the deity of Christ are really people who have been hurt and have emotional scars. Perhaps they have been offended by an overly strict parent, an immoral Christian leader, or another adult who talked the Christian life but didn't live it. If this is not the case, it's possible that they are on some prideful, intellectual kick.

Whether they profess atheism, agnosticism, militant humanism, or honest doubt, an appeal to their intellectual integrity through the "30-Day Experiment" can bring dramatic results.

If you encounter an individual who claims not to believe in God or the Bible, ask him to perform an experiment, as a matter of intellectual integrity. Give him this challenge:

"Read the Bible every day, starting with the Gospel of John. One hour a day, for thirty days. And every day begin your reading with a prayer:

SHARING CHRIST

'God, if You exist, and if Jesus Christ is Your revelation to man and He truly died for my sins, I want to know You personally.'

"If you pray that prayer every day, and read the Bible for an hour objectively—as an honest seeker of truth—I think you'll know what I'm talking about."

Let me encourage you to learn to appeal to one's intellectual integrity through the use of the 30-Day Experiment. You can use this approach in almost any situation where hostility, unbelief, or doubt is expressed. Follow the principle: *When in doubt about what to say, let God's Word do the talking.*

Other Questions and Smokescreens

Let's take a quick tour of some of the objections that may arise during a witnessing opportunity and suggested responses to them.

"I'm an atheist. There is no God."

"John, do you know everything there is to know?"

"Of course not. Even Einstein only scratched the surface of knowledge."

"Of all the knowledge in the world, what percent do you think you know? Eighty percent?"

"Oh, no! I'd do well to know 1 or 2 percent."

"All right. But let's assume that you knew 80 percent. Isn't it at all possible that God could exist in the 20 percent of all knowledge that you don't know?" (Bridge to the *Four Spiritual Laws*.)

"I believe God is in all men."

"Nancy, do you think Jesus Christ was a liar?"

"Oh, no. He was probably the most moral person who ever lived."

"If He wasn't a liar, then was He a deluded lunatic?"

"No—why do you ask that?"

"Well, there are only three choices. If He wasn't a liar, and if He wasn't a lunatic, then what He said had to be truth. As a matter of intellectual integrity, wouldn't you want to consider what He taught about man's relationship to God?" (Bridge to the *Four Spiritual Laws*.)

"Jesus was a great teacher, and a moral person. But I don't believe He was God."

Use the Liar/Lunatic approach illustrated above. Then, when explaining the three choices, say, "If He wasn't a liar, and if He wasn't a lunatic, then what He said about Himself had to be truth. He had to be who He said He was. As a matter of in-

SHARING CHRIST

tellectual integrity, wouldn't you want to consider what He taught about His relationship to God?" (Bridge to the *Four Spiritual Laws*.)

"I think if we're good people and don't hurt anyone, we'll go to heaven."

Again, utilize the Liar/Lunatic approach. When explaining the third choice, say, "...then what He said had to be truth. As a matter of intellectual integrity, wouldn't you want to consider what He taught about eternal life?" (Bridge to the *Four Spiritual Laws*, placing special emphasis on Ephesians 2:8,9.)

"I don't believe the Bible."

"Let me ask you a question. The main message of the Bible, which is unquestionably the most important literary work in history, is how a person may have eternal life. Do you understand what the Bible teaches about this?"

"I don't believe in eternal life."

"I'm not asking what you believe, but what you understand. Don't you agree that it would be intellectually dishonest to reject the world's most important book without understanding even its main message?"

Sharing the Good News

Most people at this point will guess that the way to have eternal life is through keeping the Ten Commandments or the Golden Rule, and by being honest and doing good things.

"John, that's an interesting answer, but it's the opposite of what the Bible teaches. Now I know you want to be objective and exercise intellectual integrity. Don't you think the more intellectual approach would be to investigate what the Scriptures teach on this matter? Then you can make an intelligent decision whether to accept or reject it." (Bridge to the *Four Spiritual Laws*.)

"I've seen too many hypocrites."

"Nancy, any time we look at men instead of at God we'll see sin and weaknesses. Christians are still human, and they'll still fail because God gives them freedom to choose whether He's in control or they are in control of their lives.

"Someone said, 'The church is a hospital for sinners, not a hotel for saints.' I also like the saying, 'The church is not a retail store, it's a repair shop.' That's so true—becoming a Christian doesn't mean we're perfect, just forgiven. We'll still sin, but as we allow God to control us, sin will become less and less appealing.

SHARING CHRIST

"But the important question is not 'What about the hypocrites?' Rather, it is 'What about *my* sin, and God's provision for it?' Would you like to investigate what Jesus Christ said about God's relationship to you?" (Bridge to the *Four Spiritual Laws*.)

"I go to church, serve on such-and-such a committee, and was raised in a good home."

"I realize that you have done all these things. But have you ever personally received Jesus Christ as your Savior and Lord?"

"I'm not sure."

"Would you like to be sure?" (Bridge to the *Four Spiritual Laws*.)

"I'm not interested."

"I understand. It's probably something you haven't had much opportunity to think about. But if you're like most people, it's possible that there will come a time in the future when spiritual matters do become important to you. I'd like to give you something that has meant a lot to me in this regard. Why don't you take it home and read it, and see what you think?" (Write your name, address, and phone number on the back of the book-

Sharing the Good News

let and give it to him. Challenge him to undertake the 30-Day Experiment.)

Planting the Seed

Never let objections intimidate you. Handle them in the best way you can, and guide the conversation back to the booklet. If the response is still negative, put your name, address, and phone number on the back of the booklet and leave it with the listener. You'll find that quite often, the hesitant listener will re-read the booklet and receive Christ in the privacy of his home.

Challenge him to do the 30-Day Experiment. Then pray for him, leaving the results to God. You have planted a seed for God to nurture in His perfect timing.

> *Your task is simply to obey; His is to work in the hearts of men and women with whom you share.*

So never let hostility, questions, and objections discourage you. God is sovereign—He has given you the duty and the privilege of sharing the gospel faithfully, intelligently, and lovingly—and you can leave the results to Him. Your task is simply to obey; His is to work in the hearts of the men and women with whom you share.

SHARING CHRIST

In the next chapter, we are going to look at the most important element in the life of a person who has placed his trust in Christ—growing in faith.

seven

HELPING OTHERS GROW IN THEIR FAITH

SEVERAL YEARS AGO, one of our staff members handed me a copy of *Sports Illustrated*. The picture on the cover was of the recent Heisman Trophy winner, the year's best collegiate football player.

"Meet your great-grandson," the staff member said, grinning ear to ear.

"What do you mean?" I asked.

"Well," he explained, "you led Fred to Christ, Fred led me to Christ, and I led Steve [the Heisman Trophy winner] to Christ."

What a blessing it was for me to see how one young man, whom I'd had the privilege of introducing to Jesus Christ, was already directly responsible for two generations of new believers. He had taken the training I had shared with him, then passed it along to another who in turn was discipling still another.

The discipleship process is especially important for new Christians. During the days, weeks, and months following their decision to receive

SHARING CHRIST

Christ, they will encounter doubts, conflicting emotions, and questions about what they have done. They will continue to be exposed to that same negative, humanistic world that formed their B.C. (Before Christ) worldview. Temptations will continue to hammer at them, often more intensely than before. And the people they love most may discount—even ridicule—their decision.

That's why follow-up is so vital to the new believer. He is just a babe in Christ, down from the mountaintop experience of new birth, thrust back into his hostile environment. He needs help in understanding God's love and provision for him and how living for Christ affects his daily walk.

When a mature Christian considers the value of a soul, which Jesus taught is worth more than all the wealth of the world, he will be eager to help each new Christian grow and become a true disciple.

Discipling Modeled by Christ and Paul

Our Lord could have spent all His time in evangelism. But He spent much time discipling those closest to Him, especially the twelve. He considered discipling so important that He included it

Helping Others Grow in Their Faith

in His command to fulfill the Great Commission: "Teach these new disciples to obey all the commands I have given you" (Matthew 28:20).

The apostle Paul took seriously our Lord's command. To the Colossians he wrote, "Everywhere we go we talk about Christ to all who will listen, warning them and teaching them as well as we know how. We want to be able to present each one to God, perfect because of what Christ has done for each of them" (Colossians 1:28).

In a letter to Timothy, Paul counseled, "You must teach others those things you and many others have heard me speak about. Teach these great truths to trustworthy men who will, in turn, pass them on to others" (2 Timothy 2:2).

The Multiplication Principle

While Jesus placed strong emphasis on witnessing, and the apostle Paul was influenced by His example and instructions, they did not stop there. They emphasized the importance of bringing new converts to spiritual maturity so they 1) would be strong in the Lord, and 2) would teach the things they had learned to others. Evangelism, discipleship, and spiritual multiplication were intertwined in everything the Lord Jesus, the apostle Paul,

SHARING CHRIST

and other disciples did, and this is why the early church grew so dramatically.

The same principle holds true today. In the early years of my personal ministry, I spent considerable time contemplating whether I should concentrate solely on evangelism, or pursue the dual objectives of evangelism and discipleship. After much thought and prayer, I decided that the Lord had called me to do both. So I worked intensively with those who became Christians through my ministry, to build them in their faith and to instruct them to reach and teach others. As others joined the staff, we continued to place a strong emphasis on both discipleship and evangelism.

Simply serving God was not enough. I longed to possess a heart overflowing with love and praise for my Lord.

Looking back, I'm glad I made that decision, for simple mathematics shows the wisdom of our Lord's emphasis on disciple-building. If you were to personally lead one person to Jesus Christ every day, and none of them introduced anyone else to the Lord, the result after fifty years would be over 18,000 souls for Christ. However, if you were to teach those new believers how to introduce others

Helping Others Grow in Their Faith

to Christ, and they in turn taught *their* disciples how to witness, the fifty-year result would be in the hundreds of millions. This has been the result of our emphasis on evangelism and discipleship during the last fifty years, beginning in 1951. All glory and praise belong to our great God and Savior.

Obviously, life doesn't happen quite so neatly. It often is not possible to personally disciple everyone you've introduced to Christ.

But the multiplication principle does illustrate how the world can indeed be changed through the lives of those who become true disciples. This is the goal we have sought to keep before us in the ministry of Campus Crusade for Christ, and I believe that it has been one of the keys to our growth and spiritual blessing. As of 2002, Campus Crusade has over 27,000 full-time staff and over 500,000 trained volunteer staff in 196 countries in the world.

"Follow-Up": The Initial Stage

I cannot stress enough the importance of follow-up for the new believer. "Follow-up" is a term coined to describe the vital, initial stages of discipleship. Ideally, follow-up begins within twenty-

SHARING CHRIST

four hours after the new believer's decision for Christ, and is done by either the person who led him to the Lord or a trusted Christian delegated to take on the task. If the new believer is of the opposite sex, I strongly recommend that you have a trusted friend of the same gender do the follow-up. I have often told women, for example, "I know a sharp Christian woman whose background is very similar to yours. Would you mind if I had her contact you?" This precaution can prevent potential misunderstandings and mixed-up emotions.

The discipler's job during follow-up is to provide encouragement, answer questions, and lend prayer support; to help the new believer understand and further commit himself to the lordship of Christ; to network the new convert with other Christians and a Bible-teaching church fellowship; and to help wean this "babe in Christ" from milk to solid food through a systematic beginning Bible study and a regular witnessing program.

When the Decision Is Made

When someone receives Christ with you, it is important to get his address and phone number, and give him yours. If you live in close proximity, set an appointment to get together the next day (within two days at the most). Explain that you want to give him more information that will help him as he begins his new life. Encourage him to take the *Four Spiritual Laws* booklet home and re-read it that night to affirm God's love for him and the decision he has made. In addition, he should read the first three chapters of the Gospel of John that same night. Ask him to come to the first appointment with any questions he might have.

If you don't live close by, ask for permission to call him to see how he's getting along, then call the next day. Within that same twenty-four hour period, put a letter of encouragement in the mail, along with a copy of *How You Can Be Sure You Are a Christian*, the first of eleven Transferable Concepts which are written to help the new Christian take his first steps in the faith. (The Transferable Concepts, and other recommended materials for follow-up, are generally available at your Christian bookstore. See the Resources for information.)

The First Meeting

The first meeting (or first phone call) is a time to reinforce the significance of what God is now doing in the life of the new Christian. Here is what should be covered:

SHARING CHRIST

1. Questions the new believer may have.

2. The matter of feelings. Review the train diagram on page 12 of the *Four Spiritual Laws* booklet (or one of its versions).

3. Assurance of salvation. *Ask*: "Where is Christ right now in relation to you?" Review Revelation 3:20. *Ask:* "If you were to die tonight, do you know without a doubt that you would go to heaven?" Review 1 John 5:11–13. *Ask:* "Will Jesus Christ ever leave you?" Review Hebrews 13:5.

4. Walk through the five facts on page 13, looking up and reading together the Scriptures that support each point:

- Christ has come into your life (Revelation 3:20; Colossians 1:27).

- Your sins have been forgiven (Colossians 1:14).

- You have become a child of God (John 1:12).

- You have received eternal life (John 5:24).

- You have begun the great adventure for which God created you (John 10:10; 2 Corinthians 5:17; 1 Thessalonians 5:18).

Helping Others Grow in Their Faith

5. Give him a copy of the Transferable Concept *How You Can Be Sure You Are a Christian*. Ask him to read it during the next two days, and set an appointment for another meeting (or phone call) within the next seventy-two hours. You could say, "John, it's really important that you get started properly in your walk with God. Would it be all right if we meet regularly to study the Bible together and see how it applies to our lives?"

6. If you have not done so already, encourage him to begin reading the Gospel of John preferably early in the morning, or, if not possible, at night before going to sleep. Introduce it as a historical account of the life of Jesus Christ and what His life means to us.

7. Pray together, thanking God for the salvation and new life He has brought to your friend.

The Second Meeting

Whenever possible, your second follow-up meeting should be within three days of the first. This frequency at the beginning of the discipling process will help build a sense of positive momentum in the new Christian's growth pattern, and will

SHARING CHRIST

help prevent doubts, questions, and daily problems from overwhelming him.

1. Pray together, asking God to bless your time of fellowship.

2. Ask him if he has read *How You Can Be Sure You Are a Christian*. Answer any questions he has, then go through the Self-Study Guide questions in the booklet, looking up each of the Scripture references. Encourage him to write his answers down on paper.

3. Find out how he's doing in reading the Gospel of John. You might ask, "What are the most meaningful truths you have discovered in your reading?" Do your best to answer questions (if you don't know an answer, be honest and say so; promise to get an answer to him as soon as possible). Encourage him to keep reading.

4. Give him the second Transferable Concept, *How You Can Experience God's Love and Forgiveness*. Ask him to read it through and answer the questions himself before the next meeting.

5. Invite him to church with you next Sunday. Offer a ride, and either take him to lunch or

Helping Others Grow in Their Faith

invite him home for lunch afterward.

(If you're doing follow-up over a long distance, mail your new believer the recommended Transferable Concepts and discuss them briefly by phone. Encourage him to write you with further questions and regular reports on how he's doing spiritually. Through your pastor or other reliable contacts, locate a good church in your new friend's locale and encourage him to attend. Drop the pastor of that church a note encouraging him to invite your friend to the next Sunday's activities.)

6. Pray together, and set up your next appointment for approximately one week later.

Subsequent Meetings

There are eleven Transferable Concepts, and we have found the series to be extremely effective in helping new believers. Your next several meetings could cover some or all of the remaining concepts:

How You Can Be Filled with the Spirit
How You Can Walk in the Spirit
How You Can Love by Faith
How You Can Pray with Confidence
How You Can Be a Fruitful Witness

SHARING CHRIST

How You Can Introduce Others to Christ
How You Can Help Fulfill the Great Commission
How You Can Experience the Adventure of Giving
How You Can Study the Bible Effectively

Always plan and prepare, but never let follow-up meetings be so rigid that you fail to deal with questions and concerns your disciple might have. Your main objective is to help him develop a lifestyle of love, faith, obedience, and witnessing.

Lead by Example

Let your personal enthusiasm for God and His Word be evident in your daily walk. We cannot expect others to become students of the Word unless we are students of the Word. We cannot expect them to lead others to Christ unless they see us leading others to Christ. By example, you can model practical Christian living: victory over circumstances; faith in troubled times; a godly, moral, Christ-centered lifestyle; and love, joy, peace, patience, kindness, goodness, faithfulness, gentleness, and self-control.

Obviously, however, you cannot afford to wait for inner perfection before you disciple another person. Be candid with him about your own weak-

Help Others Grow in Their Faith

nesses and struggles. Let him see you "breathe spiritually" when you fail; invite him to pray with you through tough times. You will find that, in addition to teaching by example, you will actually grow with your disciple.

Pray for Him

The Lord Jesus prayed for His disciples and for all who would ultimately believe, including us (John 17). The apostle Paul also prayed for all whom the Lord had placed in his charge. For example, in Ephesians 1:16–18 he wrote, "I pray for you constantly, asking God, the glorious Father of our Lord Jesus Christ, to give you wisdom to see clearly and really understand who Christ is and all that He has done for you. I pray that your hearts will be flooded with light so that you can see something of the future He has called you to share."

Pray daily for the new believer.

Teach Spiritual Growth

As you continue to meet with your new Christian friend, follow-up will mature into discipleship as you take him from "milk" to "solid food." Teaching the truths necessary for Christian growth in-

SHARING CHRIST

volves a number of important aspects, most of which are covered in the Transferable Concepts series. (See the Resources for information.)

What About Failures?

Often, I have shed tears of heartache and sorrow over men and women into whose lives I have poured much time and prayer, only to have them drift away to dishonor the Lord. Then the Lord reminded me that they were His responsibility. He reminded me of the Parable of the Sower, which teaches that not all seed falls on good soil. While it can be disappointing, I have learned that I need to keep on trusting God and not be discouraged in my efforts to win and build men and women for Christ. Just as successful witnessing is simply taking the initiative to share Christ in the power of the Holy Spirit, and leaving the results to God, so:

> *Successful follow-up is simply taking the initiative to build disciples in the power of the Holy Spirit, and leaving the results to God.*

Take follow-up and discipling seriously—they go hand-in-glove with successful witnessing. Never forsake a witnessing opportunity just because you don't feel you would be able to follow up on someone. You can always network a new believer to a pastor or another Christian who will work with him.

Likewise, never forsake follow-up and disciple-building with a new believer when the opportunity is there. Not only will you be helping a person grow into a mature, caring member of the Body of Christ, but you will also experience the indescribable blessing of being God's chosen workman in the process.

The Most Important Thing You Can Do

Over the years, wherever I have traveled, I have asked Christians two questions. First, *What is the most important thing that has ever happened to you?* Invariably, they answer, "Receiving Jesus Christ as my personal Savior and Lord." Next I ask, *What, then, is the most important thing you can do in life to leave a positive mark on society?* Invariably, a light goes on in the eyes of my fellow believers. "Tell others the good news—that Christ died for their sins and offers them abundant, eternal life."

Only in eternity will we know the impact of believers sharing with others, as soon as they can, the good news of Christ's forgiveness. Years ago, I was at Penn State where our staff showed me a wheel with the names of hundreds of students and staff leaders. Under each name was a list of the people whom they were discipling. They were experiencing the thrill of spiritual multiplication, according to 2 Timothy 2:2: "For you must teach others those things you and many others have heard me speak about. Teach these great truths to trustworthy men who will, in turn, pass them on to others." Some of the staff and students had as many as ten spiritual "generations" of people whom they had led to Christ and discipled, who in turn had led others to Christ and discipled them, and so on.

As for my own witnessing experiences, I indeed have counted it a privilege to reach out through my shyness and introduce others to our Savior. From the cab driver to the U.S. senator, from the blue-collar worker to the influential businessman, all are equal and precious in God's sight and all need Jesus Christ.

As I thought about these people, and of the others the Lord had brought into His kingdom through our ministry, the thought occurred to me: *You just never know, when you take the initiative to*

Helping Others Grow in Their Faith

share Christ, what will become of it.

Some may turn you down outright.

Others may express some interest, but not feel "ready."

Others may receive Christ with you, but you won't have opportunity for follow-up.

But God loves each of these people even more than you do. He is not willing that any should perish. And when you've been faithful and done your part, you can leave the results to Him.

Just as He has with all of the people mentioned in this book, He may use your obedience in sharing Him to influence generations to come.

All He expects of us is our obedience to share openly, lovingly, without reservation, the greatest news ever announced:

God loves you, and offers a wonderful plan for your life.

WOULD YOU LIKE TO KNOW GOD PERSONALLY?

THE FOLLOWING four principles will help you discover how to know God personally and experience the abundant life He promised.

1 *God **loves** you and created you to know Him personally.*

God's Love
"God so loved the world that He gave His only begotten Son, that whoever believes in Him should not perish, but have eternal life" (John 3:16).

God's Plan
"Now this is eternal life: that they may know you, the only true God, and Jesus Christ, whom you have sent" (John 17:3).

What prevents us from knowing God personally?

2 *Man is **sinful** and **separated** from God, so we cannot know Him personally or experience His love.*

SHARING CHRIST

Man Is Sinful
"All have sinned and fall short of the glory of God" (Romans 3:23).

Man was created to have fellowship with God; but, because of his own stubborn self-will, he chose to go his own independent way and fellowship with God was broken. This self-will, characterized by an attitude of active rebellion or passive indifference, is an evidence of what the Bible calls sin.

Man Is Separated
"The wages of sin is death" [spiritual separation from God] (Romans 6:23).

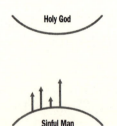

This diagram illustrates that God is holy and man is sinful. A great gulf separates the two. The arrows illustrate that man is continually trying to reach God and establish a personal relationship with Him through his own efforts, such as a good life, philosophy, or religion—but he inevitably fails.

The third principle explains the only way to bridge this gulf...

Would You Like to Know God Personally?

3 *Jesus Christ is God's **only** provision for man's sin. Through Him alone we can know God personally and experience God's love.*

He Died In Our Place
"God demonstrates His own love toward us, in that while we were yet sinners, Christ died for us" (Romans 5:8).

He Rose From the Dead
"Christ died for our sins…He was buried…He was raised on the third day according to the Scriptures …He appeared to Peter, then to the twelve. After that He appeared to more than five hundred…" (1 Corinthians 15:3–6).

He Is the Only Way to God
"Jesus said to him, 'I am the way, and the truth, and the life; no one comes to the Father, but through Me'" (John 14:6).

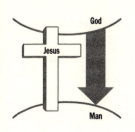

This diagram illustrates that God has bridged the gulf that separates us from Him by sending His Son, Jesus Christ, to die on the cross in our place to pay the penalty for our sins.

SHARING CHRIST

It is not enough just to know these three truths...

4 *We must individually **receive** Jesus Christ as Savior and Lord; then we can know God personally and experience His love.*

We Must Receive Christ
"As many as received Him, to them He gave the right to become children of God, even to those who believe in His name" (John 1:12).

We Receive Christ Through Faith
"By grace you have been saved through faith; and that not of yourselves, it is the gift of God; not as a result of works that no one should boast" (Ephesians 2:8,9).

When We Receive Christ, We Experience a New Birth
(Read John 3:1–8.)

We Receive Christ By Personal Invitation
[Christ speaking] "Behold, I stand at the door and knock; if anyone hears My voice and opens the door, I will come in to him" (Revelation 3:20).

Receiving Christ involves turning to God from self (repentance) and trusting Christ to come into our

Would You Like to Know God Personally?

lives to forgive us of our sins and to make us what He wants us to be. Just to agree intellectually that Jesus Christ is the Son of God and that He died on the cross for our sins is not enough. Nor is it enough to have an emotional experience. We receive Jesus Christ by faith, as an act of our will.

These two circles represent two kinds of lives:

Self-Directed Life
- **S** – Self is on the throne
- **†** – Christ is outside the life
- **●** – Interests are directed by self, often resulting in discord and frustration

Christ-Directed Life
- **†** – Christ is in the life and on the throne
- **S** – Self is yielding to Christ
- **●** – Interests are directed by Christ, resulting in harmony with God's plan

Which circle best represents your life?
Which circle would you like to have represent your life?

The following explains how you can receive Christ:

You Can Receive Christ Right Now by Faith Through Prayer
(Prayer is talking with God)

God knows your heart and is not so concerned with your words as He is with the attitude of your heart. The following is a suggested prayer:

> *Lord Jesus, I need You. Thank You for dying on the cross for my sins. I open the door of my life*

and receive You as my Savior and Lord. Thank You for forgiving my sins and giving me eternal life. Take control of the throne of my life. Make me the kind of person You want me to be.

Does this prayer express the desire of your heart?

If it does, I invite you to pray this prayer right now, and Christ will come into your life, as He promised.

How to Know That Christ Is in Your Life
Did you receive Christ into your life? According to His promise in Revelation 3:20, where is Christ right now in relation to you? Christ said that He would come into your life and be your friend so you can know Him personally. Would He mislead you? On what authority do you know that God has answered your prayer? (The trustworthiness of God Himself and His Word.)

The Bible Promises Eternal Life to All Who Receive Christ
"God has given us eternal life, and this life is in His Son. He who has the Son has the life; he who does not have the Son of God does not have the life. These things I have written to you who believe in the name of the Son of God, in order that you may know that you have eternal life" (1 John 5:11–13).

Would You Like to Know God Personally?

Thank God often that Christ is in your life and that He will never leave you (Hebrews 13:5). You can know on the basis of His promise that Christ lives in you and that you have eternal life from the very moment you invite Him in. He will not deceive you.

An important reminder…

Do Not Depend on Feelings

The promise of God's Word, the Bible—not our feelings—is our authority. The Christian lives by faith (trust) in the trustworthiness of God Himself and His Word. This train diagram illustrates the relationship among *fact* (God and His Word), *faith* (our trust in God and His Word), and *feeling* (the result of our faith and obedience). (Read John 14:21.)

The train will run with or without the caboose. However, it would be useless to attempt to pull the train by the caboose. In the same way, as Christians we do not depend on feelings or emotions, but we place our faith (trust) in the trustworthiness of God and the promises of His Word.

SHARING CHRIST

Now That You Have Entered Into a Personal Relationship With Christ

The moment you received Christ by faith, as an act of the will, many things happened, including the following:

- Christ came into your life (Revelation 3:20 and Colossians 1:27).
- Your sins were forgiven (Colossians 1:14).
- You became a child of God (John 1:12).
- You received eternal life (John 5:24).
- You began the great adventure for which God created you (John 10:10; 2 Corinthians 5:17; and 1 Thessalonians 5:18).

Can you think of anything more wonderful that could happen to you than entering into a personal relationship with Christ? Would you like to thank God in prayer right now for what He has done for you? By thanking God, you demonstrate your faith.

To enjoy your new relationship with God...

Suggestions for Christian Growth

Spiritual growth results from trusting Jesus Christ. "The righteous man shall live by faith" (Galatians 3:11). A life of faith will enable you to trust God increasingly with every detail of your life, and to practice the following:

Would You Like to Know God Personally?

G *Go* to God in prayer daily (John 15:7).

R *Read* God's Word daily (Acts 17:11); begin with the Gospel of John.

O *Obey* God moment by moment (John 14:21).

W *Witness* for Christ by your life and words (Matthew 4:19; John 15:8).

T *Trust* God for every detail of your life (1 Peter 5:7).

H *Holy Spirit*—allow Him to control and empower your daily life and witness (Galatians 5:16,17; Acts 1:8).

RESOURCES

Transferable Concepts. This series of time-tested messages teaches the principles of abundant Christian life and ministry. These messages, available in book format and on video or audio cassette, include:

How You Can Be Sure You Are a Christian
How You Can Experience God's Love and Forgiveness
How You Can Be Filled with the Spirit
How You Can Walk in the Spirit
How You Can Be a Fruitful Witness
How You Can Introduce Others to Christ
How You Can Help Fulfill the Great Commission
How You Can Love by Faith
How You Can Pray with Confidence
How You Can Experience the Adventure of Giving
How You Can Study the Bible Effectively

A Great Adventure. Written as from one friend to another, this booklet (formerly the Van Dusen letter) explains how to know God personally and

SHARING CHRIST

experience peace, joy, meaning, and fulfillment in life.

Have You Heard of the Four Spiritual Laws? One of the most effective and widely used evangelistic tools ever developed, the *Four Spiritual Laws* gives you a meaningful, easy-to-use way of sharing your faith with others.

Witnessing Without Fear. This best-selling, Gold Medallion book offers simple hands-on, step-by-step coaching on how to share your faith with confidence. The chapters give specific answers to questions people most often encounter in witnessing and provide a proven method for sharing your faith.

These and other fine products from *NewLife* Publications are available from your favorite bookseller or by calling (800) 235-7255 (within U.S.) or (407) 826-2145, or by visiting www.nlpdirect.com.

William R. Bright
*Founder, Chairman, and President Emeritus,
Campus Crusade for Christ International*

From a small beginning in 1951, the organization he began now has a presence in 196 countries in areas representing 99.6% of the world's population. Campus Crusade for Christ has more than 70 ministries and major projects, utilizing more than 25,000 full-time and 500,000 trained volunteer staff. Each ministry is designed to help fulfill the Great Commission, Christ's command to help carry the gospel of God's love and forgiveness in Christ to every person on earth.

Born in Coweta, Oklahoma, on October 19, 1921, Bright graduated with honors from Northeastern State University, and completed five years of graduate study at Princeton and Fuller Theological Seminaries. He holds five honorary doctorates from prestigious institutions and has received numerous other recognitions, including the ECPA Gold Medallion Lifetime Achievement Award (2001), the Golden Angel Award as International Churchman of the Year (1982), and the $1.1 million Templeton Prize for Progress in Religion (1996), which he dedicated to promoting fasting and prayer throughout the world.

SHARING CHRIST

He has received the first-ever Lifetime Achievement Award from his alma mater (2001).

Bright has authored more than 100 books, booklets, videos and audio tapes, as well as thousands of articles and pamphlets, some of which have been printed in most major languages and distributed by the millions. Among his books are: *Come Help Change the World*, *The Secret*, *The Holy Spirit*, *A Man Without Equal*, *A Life Without Equal*, *The Coming Revival*, *The Transforming Power of Fasting & Prayer*, *Red Sky in the Morning* (co-author), *GOD: Discover His Character*, *Living Supernaturally in Christ*, and the booklet *Have You Heard of the Four Spiritual Laws?* (which has an estimated 2.5 billion circulation).

He has also been responsible for many individual initiatives in ministry, particularly in evangelism. For example, the *JESUS* film, which he conceived and financed through Campus Crusade, has, by latest estimates, been viewed by over 4.6 billion people in 236 nations and provinces.

Bright and his wife, Vonette, who assisted him in founding Campus Crusade for Christ, live in Orlando, Florida. Their two sons, Zac and Brad, and their wives, Terry and Katherine, are also in full-time Christian ministry.